Contents

Preface

The initial research for this book was made possible by a research grant from the Association of Theological Schools. That fellowship enabled me to spend a year at the Divinity School of the University of Chicago and the Jesuit School of Theology in Chicago. The librarians of the Lutheran School of Theology in Chicago were most helpful in my research efforts. Over the next seven years, the research continued and the results were tested in lectures to students at the Jesuit School of Theology at Berkeley (JSTB) whose questions moved the project forward. The first draft of the book was written at the Jesuit Residence of the Ateneo de Manila on the typewriter of the late Bart Lahiff, S.J. When I returned to Berkeley, I began a nine-year tenure as Dean where I had the opportunity to put some of my ideas into practice. During that period two more drafts emerged: one in which the assistance of Ruth Chojnacki improved immeasurably the readability of the text; the other was written under the meticulous scrutiny of Michael Buckley, S.J. Francis Sullivan, S.J., read the final draft which Maria de Pedraza typed. Three groups of people deserve special mention in the genesis of the manuscript: the faculty of JSTB who discussed four of the six chapters at faculty colloquia; students in ST3048, "Models of the Church," who read the text in its various incarnations and made helpful suggestions; and a host of research assistants who pursued footnote queries and summarized articles and books, especially Michael Bradt who contributed so much to the compilation of the index. Many thanks to the following at The Liturgical Press: Mark Twomey, Aaron Raverty, David Manahan, O.S.B., and Colleen Stiller. Finally, I need to express my profound gratitude to Elisabeth Byrne who always encouraged me to "get on with it" and "get it done."

Introduction

In the past several years, a number of books by Roman Catholic theologians have appeared on the topic of Church authority. Two by Ladislaus Orsy[1] and Francis Sullivan[2] have concentrated on the authority of the Church's teaching offices (or magisterium).

Orsy's book attacks a distinction too often made between a teaching Church (the pope and the bishops) and a learning Church (the rest of us). He insists that the whole Church both learns and teaches. The college of bishops with the pope as its head forms a "qualified" teacher which witnesses to the faith of the whole body faithful who cannot err in matters essential to the faith. Then, in the remainder of his book, Orsy addresses the issues of assent to and dissent from official Church teaching. He reminds us that the early Church was a communion of local churches and of members of those churches bonded together in such a way that both the churches and the members were expected to give an *obsequium* to Church teaching that was more than mere respect but less than abject submission. *Obsequium* was an attitude toward such teaching rooted in a love of the Church that hoped to embrace the teaching once it was clear that it reflected and witnessed to the faith of the whole Church.

Sullivan reminds us that bishops have succeeded to the apostolic ministry of pastoral leadership in the primitive Church such that their teaching has a fullness which that of other Church members does not have. This fullness is "divinely instituted" in the sense that the Holy Spirit guided the early Church to have bishops and to heed what they were taught. Sullivan

---

[1] Ladislaus Orsy, *The Church: Learning and Teaching* (Wilmington, Del.: Michael Glazier, 1987).

[2] Francis Sullivan, *Magisterium: Teaching Authority in the Catholic Church* (N.Y.: Paulist Press, 1983).

restricts the term *magisterium* today to the teaching of the episcopal college in union with its head, the Bishop of Rome. This college can articulate dogmas that pronounce truths divinely revealed and normative for the faith of the people of God. In this articulation they possess infallibility as they are assisted by the Spirit of the Lord who guarantees the truth of what is said. Nonetheless, neither pope nor bishop has any special access to divine revelation. Both are called to witness to the faith-life of the Church.

In chapter six Sullivan makes a cogent and important argument that concrete or particular norms of the natural law cannot be objects of the Church's ordinary infallible teaching authority. While Roman Catholics ought to, if possible, form their consciences according to such moral teaching, their unconditional agreement is not required. Sullivan concludes his work with an examination of a dozen theses from the International Theological Commission which ought to guide not only the magisterium but also the response to it on the part of theologians and the remainder of the faithful. All twelve reflect the author's wisdom, especially the final thesis which describes the Church as a "colloquium" or a conversational community engaged in dialogue at every step of its discernment of what is the true faith.

More recently, Richard Gaillardetz in *Witness to the Faith*,[3] has focused on the ordinary universal magisterium of the bishops dispersed throughout the world, but as one body proposing a teaching to be held without reservation. He is particularly concerned whether such teaching can be and ordinarily is infallible. A significant portion of the book examines the history of Church teaching. Gaillardetz argues that the concept of an ordinary magisterium emerged in *Tuas libenter*, the reaction of Pius IX to the 1863 Munich Congress, and found its way into conciliar Church teaching for the first time at Vatican I.

The concept was further elaborated by Roman Catholic theologians over the next century and became a focal issue during the controversy that followed *Humanae vitae*.

Gaillardertz operates out of a communion ecclesiology which sees the bishops as leaders of local churches through public proclamation of what was previously unclear or only implicitly believed. The bishops belong to a college which can give corporate testimony to the faith of the whole Church. They do so by developing and encouraging dialogue in their own churches and with their fellow bishops and their churches around the world. In this latter dimension of the dialogue, the pope as head of the college plays a crucial role. His duty is to foster free communication

---

[3] Richard Gaillardetz, *Witness to the Faith* (N.Y.: Paulist Press, 1992).

among the local churches so that their bishops can proclaim the lived faith of the whole Church by hearing and heeding the voice of the faithful. In this act of listening, they acknowledge that the Spirit inspires the preaching, theological reflection, catechesis, worship, and daily living of Church members and, thus, builds up the source for episcopal teaching.

Thomas Rausch[4] concerns himself with the relation between the Church's official teaching and its ecumenical endeavors. He finds that the hierarchical model which generally informs official teaching conflicts with the reverence for pluralism honored in ecumenical dialogue, especially when priestly celibacy, the role of women, or Christian marriage and sexuality come up for discussion. Rausch investigates the New Testament and Church history for principles that might bridge the conflict and enable the various churches to restore unity among themselves. He hopes for a more organically and conciliarly minded Church that respects, but endeavors to reconcile, diversity. He wishes that all ecclesial bodies would understand themselves as elements of one body in a communion of churches who share responsibility for preaching the gospel and strive for renewed papal primacy that would symbolize the oneness Christ willed for his people.

Edmund Hill[5] studies the relationship between authority in the Church and its ministry. He sees present debates about this relationship torn between two options: an ultramontane one which is preoccupied with obedience to the magisterium and with papal prerogatives and another which emphasizes collegiality and the need to take seriously the objections of our separated brethren to this ultramontane view. He then explores the almost two thousand years of Church history with special attention to this millennium which has seen steady progress in the preeminence of the ministerial priesthood, especially the hierarchy, as alone endowed with authority and responsible for the Church's ministry. This development has culminated in claims for the teaching authority of the Vatican and its exclusive right to appoint bishops. Justification for these claims reached apogees in Vatican I's *Pastor aeternus* (1870) and Pius XII's *Humani generis* (1950). Hill argues that Vatican II provided a healthy antidote to the excesses of these claims and their justifications. It relativized the hierarchy in relation to the body faithful, contending that episcopal authority must be a service to the whole. It also stated that the bishops form a college with a head such that the entire college and not just the pope, has pastoral care and responsibility for the Church worldwide. One aspect of this service

---

[4] Thomas Rausch, *Authority and Leadership in the Church* (Wilmington, Del.: Michael Glazier, 1989).

[5] Edmund Hill, *Ministry and Authority in the Catholic Church* (London: Geoffrey Chapman, 1988).

involves the healing of divisions in Christ's Church. Thus, at least in theory, triumphalism was all but eliminated, juridicism much reduced, and clericalism mitigated.[6]

In contrast to the aforementioned books, this study looks at authority in the Church in all its guises and asks two questions: what is the source of authority when it is found in any community? How did authority in the Roman Catholic Church come to be as it is? In response to the first question, this study asserts that authority is not an attribute of a person, for example, the local bishop, nor of a thing, for example, the Scriptures. Authority is rather the bond experienced by all members of a community as they interact in certain relationships. Authority gives a particular identity to a community in a manner analogous to the identity an individual gains through free choices.

Authority resides in human practices that relate persons to persons or persons and things. These practices give one party in the relationship the initiative and place upon another party an obligation to heed that initiative. A human practice is authoritative wherever the rule which governs its right manner of action also stipulates why this practice is better than its alternatives.

Authority so described and analyzed is grounded in what this book (along with some other authors) calls the authoritative: the foundational beliefs and values of the community that make the group the particular community it is. As character grounds freedom in individual persons and functions as the reason why the person chooses as she or he does, so the authoritative grounds practices of authority and gives the community its norms for evaluating all particular acts of authority. In answering the first question, the method used is by and large phenomenological.

The response to the second question about authority requires an historical inquiry for reasons which will become clear at the end of chapter two. This study takes exception to others who have attempted to derive the nature of Church authority either philosophically or theologically. No, authority in the Church has taken its present shape over two millennia—two Spirit-filled millennia without doubt, but two thousand years where authority has been shaped by choices which might have been otherwise. While the author does believe that predecessors' decisions can be coercive on present conduct, he also insists that these decisions were timely (i.e., not

---

[6] Some other works on special topics might be acknowledged here: Peter Chirico, *Infallibility: The Crossroads of Doctrine* (Wilmington, Del.: Michael Glazier, 1983); J. Robert Dionne, *The Papacy and the Church: A Study of Praxis and Reception in Ecumenical Perspective* (N.Y.: Philosophical Library, 1987); Gustave Thils, *Primauté et infaillibilité du pontife Romain à Vatican I* (Leuven: Leuven University Press, 1989).

timeless) initiatives which determine the identity of the Church today through the force of tradition.

Chapter one explores a paradigm shift which has occurred in the Roman Catholic Church since the Second World War. Roughly, Church membership has shifted from an almost total preoccupation with official authority to a recognition of the necessary role charismatic authorities play in the Church. The chapter concludes that both types of authority are needed for the healthy functioning of the Church though it is essential to realize that official and charismatic authorities justify their actions and themselves according to quite different and sometimes conflicting logics.

Chapter two criticizes other studies that delineate authority as a subjective reality (an attribute of persons) or an objective one (a property of a thing). It also critiques two modern myths about authority: first, that authority is opposed to sound reasoning; second, that it is inimical to freedom and/or spontaneity. The chapter goes on to assert that authority in the Church is not ideally concentrated in any one person nor is such authority exclusively or even primarily juridical. Church authorities are endowed with an authority which is best understood as sacramental (in the sense that Church itself is a sacrament, not in the sense of seven sacraments). The pope, for instance, is most pope when he celebrates Eucharist for and preaches to a local assembly on one of his numerous trips.

Authority, as we have said, is a practice. The third chapter examines the grammar (cf. Wittgenstein) of practices which possess authority. They are human interactions in which the rule governing the way to proceed also functions to oblige one interactor in relation to another. To anticipate a bit (from a summary midway through that chapter):

> Authority, then, is a human, that is, socially shared and historically produced practice. In the practice, an obligation is laid on one party while another party is enabled to speak and/or act in the name of the community. Practices of authority are distinguished from other human practices in that the rules inherent in the practices are themselves the reasons for keeping the rules because these rules are stipulated in laws, embedded in custom, or constitute the bedrock whereby the community has its life. The transactions or communications between the parties who participate in a practice of authority both respect the agency of the parties and enhance their capacities for fuller living.

When authority is analyzed synchronically, it falls into two types: official or *in* authority; charismatic or *an* authority. When it is analyzed diachronically, it is found embedded in traditions which bear the past into the present, but also critically assess that heritage in light of the demands that the future makes on the community. Authority is grounded in the authoritative which provides norms for the legitimacy of all exercises of authority. Here it is crucial to acknowledge that trust in the traditionally given always precedes questions or doubts which arise about that tradition and generate different options in the future. Finally, the healthily authoritative community is one where dissent flourishes.

Chapter four looks at the first millennium of Christianity: New Testament understandings of authority; the ascendance of monoepiscopacy in the postapostolic era; the Church's universalist mission after Constantine's edict of toleration; the emergence of councils and synods as modes of government; claims for succession to Petrine primacy.

Chapter five begins with the turn towards centralization in Rome and a juridical understanding of ecclesial authority in the eleventh century. It also notes various challenges to these two tendencies and the Avignon Schism as well as Conciliarism which brought the conflicts to their culmination in the medieval ages. Much of the shape of authority in the Roman Catholic Church of 1999 had its origins in the Church's reactions to the Reformation. These reactions governed the development of a new branch of theology, ecclesiology, which insisted on the centrality of the papacy in understanding what Christ willed and on the visible character of his Church. With Vatican I the infallibility of the Church and of the Bishop of Rome were inextricably intertwined. At Vatican II the concentration of power in Rome and the juridical interpretation of all ecclesiastical power were gently corrected.

Chapter six, after pausing to ask whether the theory expounded in the first three chapters is consonant with the history of the development of Church authority, inquires what makes Church authority Christian and, then, Roman Catholic. It is Christian if it is under God, eschatological in character, and sacramental. Roman Catholicism accepts an episcopal college with the Bishop of Rome as its head which serves the body faithful and witnesses to the sense of lived faith in the whole Church. This chapter concludes with a number of observations on the religious freedom of the baptized, especially their right to speak freely in the Church.

CHAPTER 1

Authority in the Church: A Central Issue and Some Other Issues

Prologue

He never wanted to help out at Mass on the village's feast days. The priest from the neighboring district who came to say those Masses asked him to serve as sacristan, and frequently he demanded it. Lahuaymarca had an Indian sacristan.

"That Indian doesn't know anything; he repeats the words like a parrot, and he's almost not Christian. You're a mestizo and the organist, and you can answer in Latin. The mass will be a bigger affair with you," the priest told him the night before the big fiesta.

"I'm suffering, Father," the sacristan answered. "The Church inside my breast is burning. How am I going to be able to sing? This Gertrudis sings like an Angel."

"This Gertrudis doesn't think about God; she's too melancholy when she sings—yeah—because she's deformed."

"Look, Father, you don't understand the soul of the Indians; Gertrudis, even though she doesn't know God, belongs to God. If not, then who gave her that voice that can even wipe away sin? She consoles the sad people and makes the happy person think; she can remove the filth from any blood."

"Okay, you obstinate old fool; I can't make you; that old 'hunchback' has something— something strange—it hurts."

"It's God, Father. She's suffered among the masters. The God of the masters has no equal. He makes people suffer without letting up. . . . She's arrived all jaundiced, broken . . . without even her cap. She's come back with those same old clothes, but in her eye, there's God."

"What God? How do you know?"

"God is hope; God is happiness; God is life. When he came he was sickly, weak, and beaten down. He left firm and strong, like an eagle. He was a true man. God is here now, in Lahuaymarca. He's left the town of San Pedro, I imagine forever."

"Why, you're not even a real Christian, my child! And you've been a sacristan all these years! You think like one of the witchdoctors. God is everywhere! Everywhere!"

The old sacristan from San Pedro shook his head to say no. "Was God in the hearts of those who broke the body of our innocent school teacher, Bellido? And is God in the body of the engineers who are killing our 'Emerald Mountain'? And is God with our politicians who took away the corn fields from the rightful owners where the Virgin used to play with her Son during every harvest? Don't make me cry, Father! I'm walking around like a dead man too. God's with Don Demetrio, and he's with that 'hunchback' when she sings; God fights with the devil in Don Bruno; but for me there's no comfort—not from nobody!"[1]

A Paradigm Shift

This dialogue between the visiting priest and the mestizo sometime sacristan, presents us with a number of conflicts. They differ over who belongs to the Church, where God is found, what are the signs of God's presence, and on a host of other issues. In this essay, I will concentrate on one aspect of their difference: who has the power of and responsibility for speaking and acting in the name of the community and its God? What do we count as authoritative in Christianity? We should also admit that, in the past twenty-five years, there has occurred a dramatic shift in what we take for granted regarding authority; the change can probably be appropriately described as a shift in paradigms.[2] The term *paradigm shift,* applied to a social structure, implies decisive differences between the old and the new regarding the data and human experiences deemed to be relevant, the presuppositions which undergird argumentation, and even the foundational

[1] The passage is from Jose Maria Arguedis, *Todas Las Sangres* and is the frontispiece to the Spanish edition of Gustavo Gutierrez, *Teologia de la Liberacion.* The translation is by T. Matthew Garr, S.J.

[2] The term "paradigm shift" is from Thomas Kuhn, *The Structure of Scientific Revolutions* (Chicago: University Press, 1962). The notion has already been applied to the study of Church authority by T. Howland Sanks, *Authority in the Church: A Study in Changing Paradigms* (Missoula: Scholar's Press, 1974). The notion has been criticized by Stephen Toulmin, *Human Understanding* (Princeton: Princeton University Press, 1972) 98–123.

imagery in which the sense of what constitutes the good and the true is grounded. Let us begin our discussion of issues of authority in the Church by describing in broad strokes the paradigm shift that has taken place in the U.S. since Vatican II.

Status to Charism

First of all there has been a shift from viewing Church officials principally in terms of their status (i.e., their designated position within the institution) to viewing them primarily in terms of their charisms (i.e., the skills they actually display in their official acts, not the least of which is the skill of promoting the development of the charisms possessed by others in the community). There has been a correlative shift in the way in which response to authoritative acts is seen, from evaluation in the light of allegiance to the institution (am I a heretic or no? a schismatic or no?) to evaluation on an interpersonal basis (when I do go to Sunday Mass, do I find community there?).

Obligation to Persuasion

Secondly, our viewpoint has changed about the exercise and acceptance of official acts by both Church officials and members. Formerly, official judgments were authoritative opinions to be imposed on the Church community; and Church officials were answerable to God and higher religious authorities for the content of those judgments. For other members of the Church, acceptance of such opinions was a matter of obligation; "do I have to?" was a crucial question. Now, we see a movement towards understanding official acts as attempts to persuade both Church members and the outside world of some value which will improve the corporate life of Church members and even of the entire human community. Ratification by both Church and the world is seen to be the principal sign that an official judgment is in accord with divine will; the crucial question has become "should we want to?"

Hierarchy to Dialogue

Thirdly, in the era before Vatican II, Church authorities themselves were seen hierarchically so that a pyramid of authorities could be constructed with God at the summit, the Pope next in line, followed by bishops, clergy, religious, and laity in that order. Presently, we are moving towards a dialogue model in which all Christians are granted some participation in the divine authority through baptism, and Church officials derive their power from the body of the Church as actualized by the Spirit of God. In this context, the increasingly dominant metaphor for understanding official authorities has changed: they are no longer seen as legates or representatives of God or higher religious authorities to whom obedience is owed, but as servants of the community whose function is to foster Christlike attitudes and values, and whose responsibility is to God through the community. Furthermore, the relationship between official authority and divine dominion has altered. The will of God is not communicated simply and directly to Church officials, but through a Spirit whose activity in the Church is both complex and diverse, in other words, pluralistic.

Orthodoxy to Orthopraxis

Fourthly, before the council, Church authorities were enjoined to exercise broad jurisdictional powers and maintain orthodoxy among the faithful who were in turn expected to do and say "the right thing in the Lord." Religious authority was principally a matter of jurisdiction (a legal power of a superior over subjects) and obedience largely a matter of conformity within the community. Today, Church officials are asked to exercise their authority primarily in the celebration of the Eucharist and the proclamation of the Word and thus bring Church members to a recognition of their individual and collective need for salvation and the realization that divine forgiveness has been offered and conversion is possible. Religious authority is first and foremost a sacramental power, and obedience manifests itself in individual and communal change towards liberation.

Institution to Pilgrim People

Fifthly, the Church used to view itself as a self-contained, almost completely visible unit which had practically all the answers within its bosom. Now it seems to be grasping itself as an open-ended, in large part mystical, people who understand themselves in dialogue with nonchurch. Again, the central metaphors are different. The Church has ceased to be an anatomical body which shares in the divinity and unquestionability of its founder; it has become instead a pilgrim people commissioned by its founder to discover its authentic meaning through insertion in and confrontation with the world.

Essence to Relationality

Finally, pre-Vatican II authority in the Church was thought to be a fixed essence whose structures could be defined once and for all; the accompanying metaphors were usually physical and spatial. Now, Church authority could be better described as a relational stability in which lines of power are constantly in flux though not haphazardly; and temporal metaphors have become more appropriate.

The preceding analysis can claim at the very least plausibility; and our subsequent discussion will substantiate that it is by and large accurate. It does, however, have a number of shortcomings. First, it assumes that the office-versus-charism conflict is peculiar to religion. This is not true. The crisis of religious authority is part of a much larger crisis in Western industrialized society; the office-versus-charism conflict pervades, for example, multinational corporations as well as churches.[3] Secondly, the analysis does not take sufficient account of the historical roots of the present crisis which are deeply embedded in taken-for-granted thinking about authority today and need to be explored if we are truly to understand what is transpiring. Finally, the descriptive analysis above does not penetrate the office-versus-charism conflict to the point where its ideological components are separated from its dialectical character. At the heart of all the image-and-metaphor differences we have described lies a conflict over how we should think; and the logic of the two ways of thinking about authority in the Church described above needs to be examined in some detail. Thus, the remainder of this chapter will supplement our preliminary analysis by, first of all, examining the logics inherent in the already discussed conflicts over images of authority and reframing the office-versus-charism dispute as a dialectical relationship between structure and liminality and, then, exploring the historical roots of our present crisis as well as other issues that affect our perceptions of and responses to authority in the Church.[4]

The Logics of Office and Charism

The conflict between office and charism as the authentic basis of authority can be reinterpreted in terms of the logic inherent in the argumentation for each position. Officials usually assume that tasks in any organization are infinitely divisible and can be viewed in independence from one another; "charismatics" generally counter that such tasks are linked in networks of dependencies, and that the criterion of divisibility depends on the nature of the task and the stage of completion of the

---

[3] Cf. John Mee, "Understanding the Attitudes of Today's Employees," *Nation's Business* (August 1976) 22–28. Mee notes essentially the same changes in views of authority after studies of several corporations and his own experience in the management of a livestock company.

[4] Cf. pp. 9–11 below for an explanation of the distinction between structure and liminality. The term *liminality* refers to community as a happening or event where authority operates charismatically.

task.[5] For the former, all individuals are elements within a system, each separable from the other; for the latter, individual elements are unique and interrelated only contextually. Officials further assume that all individual elements of the organization are best related hierarchically; the best organized organization is one whose structure can be written down on paper. Charismatics, on the other hand, insist that structures are always related to the task at hand and shift over time; the demand that we be able to write all structures down on paper is akin to the assertion that the movie *Gone with the Wind* could be reduced to a set of still pictures without any aesthetic loss. Officials contend that the only relationships of significance for an organization are of a superior-subordinate type; how individuals on the same level interrelate is either inherently problematic or of no consequence. Charismatics, to the contrary, recognize no uniform type of relationship. People emerge according to the dictates of the task. Sometimes decisions are made jointly, sometimes they are entrusted to particular individuals because they alone have the necessary skills or because the group has allowed them to act thus. For charismatics, the power to make a decision and the consequent responsibility for it, however, are never permanent characteristics of an individual or status within the group. Officials are always concerned about boundaries, both the boundaries which separate the group from other groups and those which compartmentalize individuals within the group. Here definitions play a crucial role. For officials, it is of paramount importance to define who we are in contrast to others and where each of us fits into the whole system. Curiously, maintenance of such boundaries and definitions seems to require invariably an individual at the summit of the hierarchy who is unbounded and omnicompetent. Charismatics argue that boundaries are always drawn for particular purposes, and that, as those purposes change, so do the boundaries. Furthermore, they observe that official definitions often don't fit the realities of the situation. They note that the identities of groups often overlap in actual fact, and that individuals and their competencies cannot be so clearly demarcated from one another as officials would like them to be. The only boundaries which charismatics recognize as legitimate emerge as the result of the characteristics of task structure, geography, or communication. In all these in-

---

[5] By "charismatics" I obviously am not referring to members of the charismatic renewal movement in the Roman Catholic Church. I am in this section contrasting people who hold that office-holding is the paradigm for all authority with others who approach authority as if it always involves only the personal attributes of the authority figure.

stances, boundaries are related to the nature of the particular case and not the nature of things.[6]

Depending on one's taste, one will prefer either the official or the charismatic views of society and its institutions. If one prefers things like permanence, clarity, order, and a strong sense of identity, one will be inclined towards the official view. If one, however, values above all flexibility, movement full steam ahead, recognition of uniqueness, and a sense of the complexity of things, then one will opt for a charismatic perspective. Regardless of one's tastes, it is important for present purposes to recognize that societies are only humane if both views are adequately represented. Both logics are correct, but only insofar as they are being corrected by one another. When either official or charismatic logic operates to the exclusion of the other, the result is a totalitarian ideology. The consequences of such an outcome might best be shown by contrasting totalitarian and dialectical logics.

Totalitarian Versus Dialectical Logic

A logic has become a totalitarian ideology when it conceives persons to be either good or evil, but not both. Under totalitarian logic, good persons are people with good characteristics; and evil persons are those with evil characteristics. Furthermore, good persons have *only* good characteristics and evil persons *only* evil ones; such characteristics are not subject to change and are identifiable without possibility of error. If a person appears to have both positive and negative characteristics, then either the positive ones are pseudo-positive or the negative pseudo-negative. Here an interesting decision-rule emerges: since the potential costs of misidentifying an evil person are much greater than those of misidentifying a good person, persons are presumed to be evil in cases of doubt. Totalitarian logic has both an overriding goal and an overarching need. The goal is a world free of evil; and the need is for absolute and total certainty. Totalitarian logic is also nondialectical in the sense that theory always triumphs over the appearance of counterevidence; troublesome data need only be arranged to fit the theory to be properly understood.[7]

It might at first seem that the official view is more prone to becoming an ideology in support of totalitarianism than the charismatic view; history by and large bears out this intuition. The more serious danger that charismatic developments confront is evanescence. But on occasion they, too,

---

[6] The logic of the office-versus-charism conflict outlined here is based on the work of Ph. G. Herbst, *Alternatives to Hierarchies* (Leiden: Martinus Nijhoff, 1976) 17–22.

[7] Ibid. Herbst also analyzes totalitarian logic, which he calls Manichean, 74.

spawn totalitarian ideologies. When they do so, they inevitably become millenarian and define truth as like-mindedness. The group has a special vision of reality that separates it from the rest of benighted humanity. Its members conceive themselves as the vanguard of the future; they alone have seen it.

Dialectical, as opposed to totalitarian, logic has five characteristics. First, it recognizes that questions which emerge at the outset of inquiry are the result of the presuppositions of the inquirer and of the views he or she shares in common with his or her fellows. Thus, inquiry both shapes and discovers the resultant knowledge. The search for truth is a matter both of the construction of theories adequate to the subject matter and of the therapeutic destruction of those presuppositions which prove to be personal or cultural biases. Secondly, dialectical logic assumes that the real is in motion and not at rest. To represent reality as static or changeless is to do it violence. Stabilities are discoverable within the real; but they are regularities soon to change, and the real is a complexus of open forms. Thirdly, for dialectical logic reality is an admixture of good and evil. As a consequence, reality is an unstable coexistence and successive resolution of incompatible forces. The importance of this postulate epistemologically and especially for the study of history is that a dialectical logic expects that in defining itself the good will simultaneously create certain opposites which it theoretically excludes. Fourthly, the real essences of things, which are relations of contradiction and not mere regularities, are discovered by penetrating the systemic distortions which we individually and collectively impose on reality. The path towards the discernment of true essences begins with the recognition and analysis of the illusions which hold us captive. Finally, for dialectical logic, knowledge of things in their true causes consists of analogies and is often necessarily ambiguous. It must speak in analogies, examples, and metaphors because causal description is necessarily an analysis of reality in its historical concreteness. The language of dialectical logic is almost inevitably ambiguous because it attempts to capture reality in its fundamental composition as both structure and its opposite.[8] Dialectical logic is not a repudiation of such intellectual values as clarity and precision, but a relativization of their merits. The goal of its inquiry was perhaps best described by Wittgenstein: "What is most difficult here is to put this indefiniteness, correctly and unfalsified, into words."[9]

---

[8] This analysis of dialectical logic is based on Robert Heilbroner, "The Dialectical Vision," *The New Republic* (March 1, 1980) 25–31.

[9] Ludwig Wittgenstein, *Philosophical Investigations,* trans. G.E.M. Anscombe (Oxford: Basil Blackwell, 1968) 227.

Liminality and Structure

At the outset of this chapter, the issues of authority in the Church were described as a conflict between office and charism. In light of the previous paragraph we might now say that the conflict obtains between structure and antistructure. The terms this author prefers are structure and liminality.

Liminality is community as a communion of equals. It is community in its existential phase; in this phase, community is event, a happening, something going on here and now. The stress is on the centrality of personal relationships in society. The stress is also on spontaneity—that quality of human existence which brings us into contact with ourselves as nature. Liminal organization is open-ended; and its language is replete with metaphors and affectivity. For a communion of equals, God is an artist who fashioned the world out of the primeval energies lurking within the Godhead.

Anyone who has ever attended a memorable party, taken part in a protest rally, or come to the aid of a grieving neighbor knows the reality of liminality. We tell stories, shout supportive words to our comrades, or hold out a hand to our friend in need. On such occasions past and future do not matter. We strive for the empathetic response and spontaneous reactions as we approach one another on equal footing. Any organization that emerges is transitory; it does not make much difference who passes around hors d'oeuvres or makes the coffee while people at a rally really are not concerned what row they're in.

Structure is community as a society of unequals. It is community in its normative phase; in this phase, community is a differentiated and hierarchical system where individuals are situated according to the "more or less" of their talents. The focus falls on social obligations and the necessity of limits upon spontaneity. Without such limits, we would never mobilize our resources toward group goals; community would be formless. The organizations of persons in a social structure are the consequences of lucid thought and sustained will. They speak in the cognitive mode. And their God had, has, and will continue to have a plan.[10]

Structure pervades so much of human existence—in the classroom when we are young, at the office after we graduate to the world at large, and in the hospital as we take sick. The child recognizes that the teacher possesses superior knowledge, the clerk that the boss must make final

---

[10] The dialectic of structure and liminality has been described by Victor Turner, *The Ritual Process: Structure and Anti-Structure* (Ithaca, N.Y.: Cornell, 1977). First published by Aldine in 1969.

decisions, and the patient that doctors appropriately make diagnoses and prescribe treatment. In all these situations, clear explanations and well-executed plans claim our allegiance.

Both views—liminality and structure—have potential flaws.

If advocates of liminality are allowed to form community unfettered by structures, they and their companions will hold their generally small band together for a time. But, once the excitement of the beginning wears off, their destiny is structure or evanescence. These are the options unless a utopian, usually millenarian, vision takes hold of the group. Then, the call of the future may hold them together; but almost always that call, if unstructured, destroys the very ideal which gave birth to the group. Its members cease to be a communion of equals in principle open to all of humanity, and transform themselves into an elitist faction which alone sees the dawning age and knows what is moral action on behalf of what is coming. They sit in judgment on all who are outside the group. Their symbols become masks to hide how untrue they are to the ideals of liminality. Morally, anything goes if the ingroup approves it as activity on behalf of the future, even those things which history has taught us lead to degradation of the human condition.

On the other hand, if structures are allowed to be substituted for all spontaneous action, then community becomes a legalism of conventions. Such legalism destroys the *raison d'être* of all structures, for legalism homogenizes and does not preserve human differences. Under its sway, tradition ceases to be the living guide of the community. Law becomes a set of prescriptions proclaiming a god who willed us to be automatons in a system. The past is myth in the worst sense—not the story of origins which cannot be recounted in neat terms and categories, but an idealized primeval epoch where all the elements of present structures were present in all their important features. Men and women in the past are never permitted to be different from us. Legalism lives by a myth of eternal return where nothing new ever happens, happened, or can happen. And the code of rules is maintained by exceptions for certain individuals, but seldom on the basis of lucid or publicly defensible criteria.

Structure and liminality have always coexisted in Christianity. From the very first letter that Paul wrote and the very first one that a local community kept, the primitive Christian community committed the Church of Jesus Christ to structure. And every time they celebrated the Eucharist and proclaimed the Word anew, its members reminded themselves of the liminal nature of their movement. The Church of Jesus Christ is the community of a book embedded in a ritual structure and a community which celebrates sacrament and proclaims a message of liminality. As a fully human community, it combines both (structure) and (liminality). The tension between the two, whether they are described as office and charism, or structure and antistructure, is of enduring significance for the Church as a human community. The thesis, then, of this chapter is that the conflict between office and charism is best understood as the dialectical interrelationship of structure and liminality, a tension which needs to be preserved and fostered if the Church is to remain the bride of Jesus Christ, the revelation of a God who is both the source of our being and provident.[11]

The Other Issues

The principal purpose of this chapter has been to delineate an abiding problem regarding authority, namely, the dialectical tension/balance that exists between liminal and structural approaches to community. In conclusion we need to acknowledge the legacy of the Enlightenment that so affects our perception of authority today and some other factors which require our attention as we analyze the problems of religious authority in the contemporary world.

The Enlightenment: The Critical Heritage

As heirs of the Enlightenment, we live today against the background of a quite profound and often trenchant critique of authority, especially religious authority. This "coming of age" has altered drastically what we take for granted about authority and what we count as authoritative. We need to understand the issues the Enlightenment critique has raised if we are ever to make sense of our present situation.[12]

At the outset we have to take account of the fact that the Enlightenment changed the very notion of what counts as knowledge by calling for an understanding of knowledge as *criticism*. Only by continually examining and dispelling the illusions which limit our possibilities in thought and action can we transcend the insufficiencies in the present state of what we know. Before the Enlightenment, knowledge was "discovery," and the nature of the things known conditioned it. Knowledge was true if it faithfully represented the order of things external to the mind. These orders were preestablished, some by the commandment of God or the gods, some

---

[11] Avery Dulles makes a similar point about the Church in chapter two of his *A Church To Believe In* (N.Y.: Crossroad, 1982). Dulles uses the terms *Institution* and *Charism*.

[12] The roots of the present crisis have been explored by John Schaar, "Reflections on Authority," *New American Review* (VIII) 44–80. They have also been studied by David Tracy, *Blessed Rage for Order* (N.Y.: Seabury, 1975) 3–14.

because inherent in the laws of nature or of history. In any case, however, the orders existed quite independently of the human mind. The goal of human being was to bring both the self and the community into conformity with these objective orders. All known orders were presumed to be external to human knowers and constituted by forces beyond human control. In those times, authority figures ruled on the assumption that they knew the order of things. Now, after three centuries of relentless questioning, we are left with several different kinds of orders, all of which are the creations of human wills. And the rewards and punishments which order brings are all internal to the system (where the system rather than external forces creates the order). We live in a world where human harmony results from human making, and responsibility is in large part a matter of owning up to what we have done, and not of acknowledging a force outside ourselves. In this world, the central concern about authority is law and order with a vengeance: what rules of human conduct will we construct so that we can live in harmony with one another and draw from the system the maximum number of benefits for the greatest number of people like ourselves?

Since the Enlightenment, our notion of what is ethical behavior has also changed. Obedience to a tradition and its values, customs, and so forth is no longer acceptable as an ethical stance. The preferred loyalty is to critical assessment of the evidence, and the moral ideal is the hard-nosed skeptic whose inquiry is open-ended and whose search results in autonomy. Pre-Enlightenment morality was a corporate morality where community customs determined the limits of propriety as well as the boundaries of belonging: either accept the way we do things or find another tribe. Authorities in such communities (which we presumptuously call "primitive") were founders and prophets. The former created the traditions, foundational values, and customs of time immemorial; the latter summoned the community to correct certain abuses in the name of traditions, values, and customs which all agreed were right and just. But, whether they were founders or prophets, authority figures were mediators between the gods (or reasonable facsimiles thereof) and ourselves. They exercised authority because they could reenact and reaffirm the harmony that existed between an ontological order and the human realm. Their overriding conviction was that the quest for human identity, whether individual or in solidarity with others, was inseparable from legitimation in terms of a reality independent of and beyond the control of human beings. Today custom is no longer a crucial determinant of moral limits in society; and received opinion (at least if the opinion comes from parents or their ancestors) is as likely to be rejected as accepted. Instead, the person who would be moral is likely to see authentic moral behavior as inevitably requiring a separation from the group. The cherished moral consciousness has been individualized. The issue in moral authority has, therefore, become: how can we be conscious and individual, yet share in the bonds and limits of community? Are all social and collective commitments self-imprisonments?

Finally, the Enlightenment has created an existential predicament for us: what counts as genuinely real? What about our lives, thoughts, and actions has lasting significance? And, in regard to religion, can any interpretation of the supernatural ever pass muster if judged by the standards of knowledge and action of our secularized culture? The rational for us who assume empirical method to be the cornerstone of all valid knowledge follows certain specified and objective rules and procedures. Problems are carefully defined, and solutions to such problems are most often techniques which involve rearrangement of the elements that surfaced in the defining process. The reasonable individual is one who combines in his or her inquiry the values of noninvolvement, anonymity, and efficiency. The ideal society is one dominated by neutral observers who coordinate their efforts to get the job done. Basic ends and procedural assumptions have taken-for-granted status; the questioning of such ends and assumptions is regarded as both heretical and wasteful. Instrumental values constitute the rational; most personal and social problems are matters of reprogramming and reorganization. In such "rational" societies, action for the good of the whole is achieved through automation and depersonalization of all process. The whole in question is almost always seen as a cluster of parts which can be broken down and then arranged according to the similarities of the parts. In societies governed by such assumptions, the criteria of good performance in any official capacity are threefold: (1) all cases which come before the responsible authorities are to be treated without regard for any individual idiosyncrasies involved (the good bureaucrat is, in principle, objective and impersonal); (2) the highest expectation of any official is that she or he, in the conduct of office, will be detached from all personal feelings (feelings are subjective and to be left in the home); (3) in theory, at least, any official is just another cog in the machine—replaceable by any other individual who knows the rules and possesses the requisite skills for their execution.

Now what is missing from such a "rational and good" society? Only about half of what we know as life—things like conscience, intuition, empathy, dreams, and, by and large, common sense. The "unseen" hand is not only Adam Smith's ideal regulator of the free market; it is also our ideal of authority. People who cry on the steps of small town newspapers are not fit to lead our countries. Everyone knows that feelings are not objective. People who exhibit them in public are out of contact with reality. Let them weep at home.

Quite obviously this critique of authority since the Enlightenment has been sketched in rather bold, often exaggerated, strokes. There never has been a wholly traditional society in which human harmony was simply a matter of conformity to external order, long-standing customs went unquestioned, and dreams replaced all rational analysis of wholes into parts. And all our post-Enlightenment attempts at a brave new world constructed by individuals responsible only to themselves for their orders and consisting exclusively of mechanized processes have foundered against the protests or, at least, the apathy of people with sense. It is true, however, that tendencies inherent in the Enlightenment critique have left us with a certain heritage. We are suspicious of any order not of our own making, regard inherited customs and received opinions with jaundiced eyes, and presume that feelings, emotions, and the like are not objective. Too often we are forced to acknowledge our blindness to the dangers of analytic reasoning, autonomous processes, moral individualism, and the independent will responsible only to itself. These suspicions and blindness, however, have another impact which is highly significant for the present study. They make it very difficult for us to understand and assimilate the lessons that history and our traditional societies teach us about the nature of authority. And they profoundly alienate Christians from the meaning of authority in the New Testament, documents issuing from a traditional society which, albeit untutored by Sigmund Freud, still knew that dreams provided significant information. Further consideration of the lessons of history will have to be left to a subsequent chapter. Suffice it to say for now that many of our problems in grappling with issues of authority in contemporary societies are the results of historical development over the two hundred years since the Enlightenment.

A Legacy of Suspicion

First of all, as we have already noted, there has been over the last two centuries an ongoing, often bitter, critique of authority in general. One pole of this critique, which originated with the Enlightenment, has made the point that authority is inimical to solidly grounded knowledge because it is based on beliefs and opinions. Authority may sometimes have its place; it seems suitable for parents to possess authority over their children, and civil authorities must exercise jurisdiction over criminals. But authority plays a very small role in the lives of mature, responsible people. Such people have learned to question the traditional truisms and to base their knowledge on data and evidence. The other pole, which has its origins in nineteenth-century Romanticism and has most recently appeared in the guise of the New Left, has objected that authority is necessarily opposed to the unfettered spontaneity that is required for authentic freedom. Authority invariably places limits on spontaneous expressions of freedom and thus prevents individuals from actualizing themselves and collectivities from discerning the common will.

Both these critiques assume that authorities are always rigid, pledged to the mindless and insensitive repetition of the past. For them, the source of power that authority figures have is the superstition and fear of the masses. All authorities are coercive and manipulative. Their task is to convince the "great unwashed" that the common good is identical with the benefits of the traditional but outmoded order serving the interests of a privileged class.

The result of two hundred years of such critique is that the popular mind has become instinctively suspicious of all authority figures, including religious ones, and their exercise of power. Often authorities and their actions are condemned without a fair hearing. This persistent, and occasionally trenchant, critique has led one of our most prestigious and astute analysts of modern culture to suggest that authority has ceased to be a tenable notion in our time.[13]

Pluralism

Secondly, in the aftermath of each of the two world wars, we have experienced a breakdown of the consensus in Western culture in regard to values. The consensus which held the West and other parts of the world dominated by it together for several centuries appears to be a thing of the past. Political oppositions seem to run ever deeper; pluralism on ethical issues is the order of the day; ideological allegiances and alliances change with frightening rapidity. The Roman Catholic Church has not been immune to this process. It, too, has undergone a profound transformation in the network of values which holds it together as a community, especially since Vatican II. That the Church has been profoundly affected in this regard should not surprise us. When cultural values are called into question, it is the value-bearing institutions of the culture which bear the brunt of criticism. Schools, churches, and their like are judged by the highest standards and found wanting.

National Insecurity

Thirdly, people look to the state to provide them with security, both economically and militarily. But any regular reading of the daily newspaper reveals how little control nation states now possess over the national economy. Banking, industry, and commerce in general have taken on an international

---

[13] Hannah Arendt, *Between Past and Future* (N.Y.: The Viking Press, 1954) 91–141.

character, and, even when based in a particular country, they often operate according to interests in conflict with those of the home nation. One thinks of the way in which budget deficits today have variable global impacts depending on the flow of international dollars in or out of the particular country involved. A more serious problem for nation states is the bomb. Even with the end of the Cold War, no nation on the earth today can fully assure its citizens that they are safe militarily. As long as nuclear weapons exist, a government, in the final analysis, can promise only a balance of terror where the rule seems to be that though we cannot protect our own citizens from serious harm, we can inflict equal or worse harm on theirs.[14] Because they really cannot provide economic or military security in any traditional sense of those terms, nation states are inevitably weakened in regard to the allegiance they can expect from their constituents. Institutions and the officials who govern them never operate in a vacuum. A crisis of confidence in civil institutions and their officials affects all other institutions and people in a given society. And so people nervous about their money and their borders eventually turn their glance towards the Church and ask whether the latter can make them secure with God.

Change as a Permanent Feature of Human Existence

Finally, the pace of change in our world has increased at a rate unimaginable a century ago. Parents today share center stage with television (and the world opened up therein) in the rearing of their children. As children grow up, parental values are frequently tested against those of their peers and rock stars. The same children often have opportunities to travel (with or without their parents) which were the exclusive prerogative of the super-rich at the beginning of this century. All this technological change and its consequences for child-rearing could be ignored, save for the fact that the Church has regularly looked to and expected parents to inculcate the religious values the Church treasures. Wherever several agencies compete to socialize the individual, the influence of each one is lessened.[15] In our pluralistic culture both parental authority and the nurture

[14] "The general decline in authority which has been discussed is particularly marked in this area, because states are no longer able to provide the security which has been considered a mainstay of the public's acceptance of government. Not only authority but legitimacy. . . have been corroded by the threat of nuclear war." Carl Friedrich, *Tradition and Authority* (London: Pall Mall, 1972) 72.

[15] Peter Berger has pointed out how agencies of socialization in competition with one another inevitably weaken the impact that each one has on the persons being socialized. Cf. *The Sacred Canopy* (Garden City, N.Y.: Doubleday, 1967) chs. 5–7, and *A Rumor of Angels* (Garden City, N.Y.: Doubleday, 1969) chs. 1–2.

in religious values the Church presumes can no longer make the kinds of impressions on the young which were taken for granted in the past. We can only conjecture, therefore, that the future of religious authority will have to take into account that the undergirding consensus which makes religious authority feasible will be partial and that all exercises of religious authority are going to be increasingly subject to debate.

CHAPTER 2

What Authority (Secular or Religious) Is Not!

Introduction

In Number 115 of the First Part of the *Philosophical Investigations,* Ludwig Wittgenstein says, "A *picture* held us captive. And we could not get outside of it, for it lay in our language and language seemed to repeat it to us inexorably."[1] Wittgenstein was calling our attention to the fact that, in philosophical speculation, we often cannot get a clear and correct view of certain phenomena because our ordinary ways of looking at them blind us to true reality. In response, he developed a method for delving deeply into these "sicknesses" of our language and showed how insight into these cul-de-sacs in our thinking actually yielded apertures to the clear and correct view.

I propose to do something similar to what Wittgenstein did in the *Investigations.* I intend to look more carefully at some standard definitions of and attitudes toward authority. And I do so for two reasons. First, the reader's mind needs to be cleared of several false conceptions of authority. Secondly, the refutation of these false conceptions will show the way to a more adequate grasp of authority.

Authority Is Not Opposed to Rationality

At the outset, we need to turn our attention to two shibboleths of modernity: that authority stands in opposition to reasonable inquiry, and that it stands opposed to freedom and spontaneity. The former has been a long-standing objection to authority since the Enlightenment. The argument against authority runs something like this: authority is based on beliefs, and beliefs are like opinions; they are hypothetical in character. While

[1] Ludwig Wittgenstein, *Philosophical Investigations,* trans. G.E.M. Anscombe (Oxford: Basil Blackwell, 1968) I:115.

authority is useful in the rearing of children or in dealing with recalcitrants or the ignorant, it is not fitting for mature, thoughtful human beings. For this last group, all knowledge needs to be based on authenticated evidence, and this kind of evidence is gained only through the arduous process of questioning and doubting what authorities tell us is the case. We need to test what we are told for ourselves through some mode of experimental method. Authority may have been appropriate for primitive civilizations, but not for ourselves "come of age." All authority is radically irrational and grounded in faith or superstition.[2]

If we heed Santayana's dictum that those who do not know the past are condemned to repeat its mistakes, we should be suspicious of the above argument from the very start. Anyone with a sense of history (or of the *whole* world in which we live today) knows that most cultures and civilizations prior to the modern period (and the vast majority of the present world outside of our Western industrialized societies) put a high premium on authority and tradition. It is the peculiar hubris of modernity that it conceives of reasoning as rootless, that is, as severed from its foundation in authority and tradition.[3] Modernity presumes that everything can, or at least in principle should, be subjected to doubting and questioning. Only the life based on thoroughgoing and consistent skepticism is worthy of the adult human being.

Yet common experience shows that the entirety of our lives is founded on trust. We go to sleep in the confidence that our lovers will not go berserk during the night and bash in our heads. We also trust that the roof will not cave in or the floor vanish from under us. We rise in the morning confident that no one has substituted deadly gas for our shower water or poisoned our cereal. All the human activities that make up our days rest upon the assumption that others can and ought to be trusted. Doubts do occasionally arise. But it is essential to note their occasional character. Furthermore, reasonable doubts are always specific. They isolate a particular item out of experience, and question that item in the light of other things known for certain. These things are certain not because they have all been proved so beyond a shadow of a doubt, but because they are accepted as such by "reasonable" people in our culture. Thus a person reared religiously in growing up may come to have doubts about the existence of God or question the truthfulness of the religious community to which she or he has heretofore belonged. But those doubts arise against the background of what

[2] David Tracy has analyzed this phenomenon in the first chapter of his *Blessed Rage for Order* (N. Y.: Seabury, 1975).

[3] Hans-Georg Gadamer, *Truth and Method*, ed. and trans. Garrett Barden and John Cumming (N. Y.: Seabury, 1975) esp. 235–74.

is taken for granted about how any decent person, including a divine one, ought to act in certain situations, or they occur in the context of what we all accept about how a humane community should nurture growth towards adult thinking and acting. People who doubt everything are not paragons of human reasoning but rather diagnosed as paranoid.[4]

The customary ways of thinking and acting, along with the background of things to be counted as trustworthy, are the products of the history of the civilization in which we find ourselves. We are socialized into these ways and their contexts from childhood on, the process continuing throughout the whole of our lives.[5] Many of these customs were once tested and found to be trustworthy. And some of them still need to be subjected to rigorous scrutiny. But the history of our occasional need for testing custom should not blind us to what is fundamental about our human situation, namely, that reasonable people are able to lead rational lives because they place profound faith in what their ancestors have bequeathed to them. The traditions which bear us along are bodies of shared memories, images, ideas, and ideals that link the past, present, and future into a meaningful whole and provide us with orientations in the present and directions for the future. Without traditions our lives would not be grounded in meaning, nor would they have any purposes.[6]

Finally, it is important to note the ideological component of the ideal of reason recommended by the Enlightenment. The Enlightenment put forward as an exemplar of reason the autonomous individual thinker dependent on no one and isolated from all others. What we are not told is that this ideal of thinking alone in one's library apart from the cares of the world and dedicated to doubting everything is made possible by the labors of others not sovereign over their existence. The leisure to doubt *ad infinitum* enjoyed by "modern" thinkers is purchased at the price of the social and economic oppression of others. This blindness to the social sources and consequences of certain ideals of thinking makes it understandable why the Enlightenment recommendation has not issued in a culture characterized by its maturity of reflection and prudence in action, but rather in people who are narcissistic and know community only as conformity to what is banal. The present state of Western society suggests that where authority is condemned in the name of rationality, indulgence in comfort and enslavement to fashion become the rules of human behavior.

---

[4] Ludwig Wittgenstein, *On Certainty,* eds. G.E.M. Anscombe and G. H. von Wright, trans. Denis Paul and G.E.M. Anscombe (Oxford: Basil Blackwell, 1969).

[5] Anthony Giddens, *Central Problems in Social Theory* (Berkeley: University of California Press, 1979) 128–30.

[6] John Schaar, "Reflections on Authority," *New American Review,* VIII:56.

None of the above is meant to excuse those abuses of authority which have given the very genuine impression that authority is inimical to human reasoning. More often than we care to recall, rigid and irrational adherence to the way things are has been justified as God's will, the nature of things, the wisdom of the ancestors, etc. Such wooden insistence upon traditional ways of thinking and acting is in no way fidelity to authentic tradition, which is always a living and evolving reality. That authority has frequently been summoned to prevent reason from pursuing its legitimate path to truth is a fact that will need to be attended to in this study. Suffice it to say for the present, however, that authentic authority and real rationality are never opposed to one another.

Authority Is Not Opposed to Freedom or Spontaneity

The other indictment that modernity makes against authority is that it is opposed to freedom and spontaneity. This indictment comes from modern romanticism, and is usually associated with the name Rousseau. The charge runs something like this. Freedom and spontaneity, if they are to be the parents of human creativity, need to be unfettered. The artist, for example, needs to try out several alternatives and to let the imagination have free rein. Authority, which always sets limits on expressions of spontaneous urges and human liberty is, therefore, inimical to the spontaneity and freedom necessary for the creation of what is best in us.

The first objection to the above argument is that it views freedom ahistorically and antisocially. Any person with a sense of his or her own past knows that free choices always take us in one direction and not another. Freedom is not the capacity to choose everything and anything at all times, but the disciplined and reasoned rejection of some alternatives in favor of others. The free human being has cultivated prudence and forethought, and is not the one who follows the urge to do and achieve all. The free person is in debt to the past (knowing how it has made him/her the determinate person he or she is) and responsible for the future (not interested in actualizing all potentialities, but those which constitute our human glories). Freedom knows not only the urge to do things differently, but also the self-imposed limitations on freedom in the present as a result of choices made in the past. While freedom is individual autonomy, that is, liberation from both external constraints and internal inhibitions, it is also something more. Some free actions, and often the most humanly significant ones, can only be realized in solidarity with others.[7] One thinks here of civil liberties, economic opportunities, and religious worship. All these freedoms re-

---

[7] Michael Buckley, "Authority," *Agora* (Autumn 1968) 26–30.

quire the cooperation of others and the exercise of public choice. For these freedoms to be realized, we need not simply the non-interference of others, but also their participation in common enterprises. The creation of the order which such participation presupposes is the work of authority.

The argument from freedom and spontaneity against authority also takes a naive stance on human being. It assumes that all free self-actualization results in good, and that the expression of spontaneous urges is inevitably beneficial. History teaches us that while freedom and spontaneity often issue in the good and the beneficial, they sometimes bear fruits which can only be described as malevolent. The exercise of one person's self-actualization may be profoundly injurious to another, and spontaneous urges have often been the source of our worst misdeeds. As we grow older, we learn to our dismay that things which we once did according to our best and seemingly most noble lights have often brought others and eventually ourselves to grief. Many of our most seriously misguided deeds have appeared at the time to have their origin in what we deemed best about us. A healthy suspicion of freedom and spontaneity is the mark of the person who is maturely free and genuinely spontaneous.[8]

Finally, this argument against authority misconstrues how the artist works. Artists are people who have mastered a craft. They create the beautiful and express what is deeper within us against the background of deep mastery of that craft and concerted efforts to choose some alternatives and not others, to let certain urges flow freely and not others. No artist is under no obligations, follows no conventions, or recognizes no rules. He or she is always well-schooled in the traditions of his or her craft, and innovates against that background.[9]

None of this refutation is meant to justify those abuses of authority where freedom is unduly restricted or even quashed, where spontaneity is either discouraged or even repressed. That history displays too many instances where authorities were anti-liberty, anti-body, and anti-creativity is a datum for any authentic analysis of authority. Wherever authorities strive to make all free choices and spontaneous urges conform to preconceived standards or require loyalty to themselves as the supreme good, they no longer possess authority in any but the minimal legal sense. The purpose of authority is to respect, promote, and enlarge human freedom and spontaneity by assuring that free actions and spontaneous expressions are mutually enriching in a given social setting and guided by reasonable

---

[8] John Schaar, *Escape From Authority* (N.Y.: Basic Books, 1961) 284–324.

[9] Carl Friedrich, *Tradition and Authority* (London: Pall Mall, 1972) 82.

ends. The task of authority is the achievement of communities where people are self-actuated, intentional, purposive, and rational.

Authority Is Not a Subjective Reality

It seems to me that, in general, philosophical and theological studies of authority have often made the mistake of confusing authority with authorities, whether the latter be certain human subjects such as duly elected or appointed officials, or certain human objects such as sacred texts.

Numerous studies of authority have defined authority as a person or a quality of a human person.[10] An official in a hierarchy, for example, not only has, but is an authority. Or a person who, though he or she has no official status, displays particular talents and gets others to follow him or her on the basis of those talents, is also an authority. Defining authority as a person tends to overlook that people who possess authority, whether official or charismatic, do so because of entitlement. The human customs and practices of a community entitle them to be bearers of authority.[11]

Thus some individuals do have authority in our societies by virtue of their holding a particular office. They receive this authority upon assuming that office, and retain it until they are replaced in office or the office is legislated out of existence or, in extreme cases, they forfeit the right to remain in it. Such offices and the norms by which performance in office is evaluated, however, are human creations. We create offices and the hierarchies which include them. We do so in order to impose some order on what would otherwise be a chaotic human existence. And we impose those orders with particular purposes in mind, and those purposes in turn beget the norms by which the performance of a particular individual in a certain office is judged.[12] Some norms are minimalistic; that is, they stipulate the minimal conditions under which an official retains his or her position. For instance, Richard Nixon had little moral authority left as president of the United States at the beginning of August 1974. Nevertheless, he was still legally president, and the acts of his final days were binding on his successor and the nation. I doubt if anyone, no matter how critical of Nixon, would have refused to cash a tax refund because it was signed by him on his last

---

[10] Examples of this approach can be found in Walter Molinski, "Authority," *Encyclopedia of Theology (A Concise Sacramentum Mundi),* ed. Karl Rahner (N.Y.: Seabury, 1975) 61, and the article "Authority," Karl Rahner and Herbert Vorgrimler, *Theological Dictionary,* ed. Cornelius Ernst, trans. Richard Strachan (N.Y.: Herder & Herder, 1965) 44.

[11] John Schaar, "Reflections on Authority," 49.

[12] Ibid., 51.

day of office. Not all of our norms, of course, set legal minimums. We have also manifold criteria for assessing whether officials exercise their authority well, and we hold the occupants of all offices, elected and appointed, accountable to these norms. So, we prefer presidents who move the nation in one direction or another to those who merely keep the ship of state afloat.

We need to notice here that both the offices in our societies and the norms by which their exercise is evaluated are social constructions. The principal thesis of this book is that the meaning of authority is best situated in that process of social construction and the human interaction which constitutes it. While individuals who occupy official positions can rightly be called authorities, it is important to realize that they are called so by derivation. Authority properly belongs to the community which authorizes persons to act in its name.

Some people also seem to have authority in virtue of their talents. While they are accorded no official status, people spontaneously attribute authority to and follow after them. However, the talents or skills that make some persons attractive to us and propel us to become their followers are socially and historically conditioned. Today an almost necessary skill for getting elected president of the United States is the ability to get one's message across on television. Television personalities generally, because they get the message across effectively, play an important role in forming the values of our country today. In the fourteenth century the French nation followed a young girl into combat and liberated themselves from English domination because she had been called to lead in battle by the voices of her favorite saints. Today we would probably place her under a physician's care.[13] Thus, the talents which give rise to charismatic leadership and its concomitant authority have been and are evaluated differently according to the historical epoch. Moreover, in particular subgroups of contemporary society, valued charisms can differ enormously. In some groups, charismatic authority is accorded to people who are outgoing, spontaneous, and venturesome; in other groups, it is gained by those who are reserved, cautious, and judicious. The community assigns charismatic authority where its ideals of personal identity and maturity are best realized. In that assignation we find the locus of authority in the community.

The principal problem with definitions of authority which see authority as synonymous with individual persons is that they encourage license in the exercise of authority. As long as authority is not understood to be situated in entitlement by and accountability to the community, the individual

---

[13] The example, of course, is based on a remark attributed to Michel Foucault.

who acquires an office or possesses the valued skills is not bound to the purposes and values of the community. Authority then becomes instead literally what authority figures can get away with. Their acts must be presumed authoritative even when they seem opposed to what reflective and judicious people deem proper. The issue for the person in authority is not whether a particular act is conducive to the common good, but how it can be properly packaged.

Authority, then, needs to be analyzed as a communal, social, and historical reality. Forgetfulness of any of these aspects can lead to misunderstanding authority as an attribute or property of an individual person, and such definitions are not only confused and untrue, but dangerous because they render the criteria for assessing proper performance in office or appropriate use of talents private and arbitrary. Eventually, proper performance and appropriate use become what the mind of the individual performer or user wants them to be.

Authority Is Not an Objective Reality

Another mistake often made is defining authority as some object or other and speaking of these products of human labor as authorities. Religious groups, for example, often speak of their sacred texts as *the* book, that is, the authority in and for the community.[14] Nation states frequently ascribe authority to the foundational documents of the people such as constitutions, political tracts, or the like. Sometimes the laws of states are called authorities. And we even speak of the authority of a particular command or directive.

We need to attend here to the fact that such "authorities"—whether books, documents, laws, or commands—are always received within the broader context of the uses to which the community puts them. For the Christian, the Scriptures are not authoritative in themselves, but insofar as they reveal the salvific will of God in Jesus Christ. Thus, Paul's words on justification have a more permanent authority for Christians than his directives for veiling women in church since justification is more closely tied to the core. Constitutions are interpreted according to the mind of the founding fathers whose intentions are partly a matter of historical research and more so a construal of presiding judges. Laws have always been subject to a higher authority: are they in accord with the will of God, the will of the legislator, or the will of the people? Finally, particular commands

---

[14] A number of discussions of authority from the Protestant perspective speak of the authority of *the* book: Edmund Farley has surveyed these views and explored the problems to which they give rise in his *Ecclesial Reflection* (Philadelphia: Fortress, 1982).

and directives are judged according to commonly accepted standards: is *x* within the scope of *b's* authority? Is *x* a good thing to do? This broader context which gives meaning to these objects and in terms of which they are evaluated and interpreted is the "place," so to speak, where authority exists.

There is an almost automatic tendency in our Western, technological culture to look on objects apart from their uses for human purposes. When we think of a hammer, we think first of a hammer hanging in a basement workshop, and not of a hammer being used to drive a nail into the wall so that the portrait of a loved one can be hung there. When we think of the Psalter, we think initially of a book lying on a table and gathering dust, and only afterward of a worshiping community chanting "The Lord is My Shepherd" in praise of God. Thinking of important things exclusively in the objective mode and ignoring the individual or community that makes the thing important invariably misleads us and, when we do so in regard to authority, our attention is diverted from seeing the central importance of human interaction, whether with one another or with the tools we use, in grasping what authority is.[15]

A noteworthy corollary to this conception of objects as tools understood according to human purposes is that the objects undergo change in reference to the uses to which they are put. The text of Romans as read by Lutherans, by other Protestant groups, by Roman Catholics, or by an agnostic historian of religions is not exactly the same book. We do better to look on books like Romans not as inert things unaffected by human usage, but as objects altered by each different use. Romans is better viewed as a set of siblings than as a single thing ever the same. The Lutheran usage is a brother to the Protestant use, and the Roman Catholic reading is sister to them both. To say that a text has several uses is to say that it is not always exactly the same text. The text does of course have a continuous existence, but this continuity is best described as a family of uses and not as an essence only accidentally affected by usage.[16]

Regarding books, documents, laws, and commands abstracted from the context of human interaction can have pernicious consequences. First of all, what is clear and precise about objects in themselves is regularly emphasized to the detriment of what is vague and ambiguous about them in characteristic human use. Clarity and precision are laudable human goals, but when they sweep away all vagueness and ambiguity, we no longer have authentic human existence. Secondly, focusing exclusively on the object

---

[15] Martin Heidegger, *Being and Time,* trans. John Macquarrie and Edward Robinson (N.Y.: Harper and Row, 1962) 69–71, 83–86, and 360–64.

[16] The notion of "family resemblances" is from Wittgenstein.

tends to atomize what the object is. Thus it is not the Scriptures as a whole but the individual verses that command our attention. It is not the foundational document itself, but the individual articles in it that count. It is not the whole law, but a particular statute that is cited. Ultimately such preoccupation with the object in itself aims at reducing all human intercourse to a letter, thus quenching the spirit behind that letter.

A Comment

In religion, the definition of authority as either a particular subject or a produced object has had some significant consequences. Such definitions are, I believe, the principal reason why bearers of authority in religion, whether subjective or objective, are turned into idols. Authority figures become substitutes for God, believed to possess authority directly from God with no reference to community purposes and values and responsible to no one in the exercise of that authority. The sacred books, or better particular verses in those texts, become sayings direct from the divinity with no advertence to the dialogic character of those sayings (which implies human hearers as well as a divine sayer) or to the interpretative element in such sayings (which implies reference to the particular verse in the whole of the book for its meaningfulness). The only proper context for understanding religious authority is the dialogue between God and a people, where God is present as revealer and the people as hearers of and responders to that revelation. Otherwise, religious authority has no context.

The Ideal of Authority Is Not Its Totalization

Another error that is frequently made concerns the ideal rather than the nature of authority. The ideal authority is, as it were, a single person or an individual book which contains all authority.[17] From the subjective point of view, the ideal authority is a single official or charismatic individual who possesses all authority in himself or herself and shares that authority with others in the community only by his or her delegation. The inverse of this view is the sovereign autonomous underling who reserves the right to judge all acts of authority by his or her own lights. From the objective vantage point, all authority is vested in the sacred book, the founding document, the law, etc. The inverse of this view is the divine right of the private interpreter. The phrase "divine right" is appositely employed here because

---

[17] That this ideal of authority is a special characteristic of religious authority in our times has been discussed by Paul Edwards, "The Myth of Authority," *The Way* 12 (1) (1972) 186; that the same ideal operates in the secular sphere is certainly implied by Richard Sennet, *Authority* (N.Y.: Alfred Knopf, 1980).

both vantage point and its inverse arrogate the authority that belongs to God alone. Both views overlook the relational dimension of human authority. Forgotten is the fact that there are no superiors without subjects who receive the exercises of authority, no meaningful books without interpreting communities, and no individual judgments apart from the standards of the community. Genuine authority is always vicarious.[18] That is, it is held under and responsible to God or under and responsible to the common good of the people.

Forgetfulness of this relational dimension can and often does lead to serious consequences. Authorities who forget their authority is from God soon substitute themselves for the absent divinity. Those who fail to remember that the origin of their authority is in the will of the people toward the common good inevitably lead the people according to their darkest impulses. And those who forget that the mind of the founders is a social construction soon turn the foundational documents into words from the gods themselves. The journey from the totalization of authority in a single subject or object to tyranny is short.

All genuine authority is shared and collegial. It is shared in the sense that authority resides in the collective skills and talents of all the members of a community. It is collegial in the sense that the authority of the community is the sum total of all those skills and talents operating in concert.[19] Christian authority, on the other hand, is also representative and characterized by service. It is representative because it replicates the basic structure of conversation between God and the Church. It is service because it is grounded in the conviction that all who are granted authority in the Church are sinners who have been called through no merits of their own to be disciples of Jesus Christ and, consequently, know that their identity outside of grace renders them the least of the brothers and sisters.

Christian Authority Is Neither
Primarily nor Exclusively Juridical

Christian authority is not primarily juridical. It is first and foremost sacramental. Thus, the pope is not most pope when he is issuing orders through the Vatican bureaucracy, pronouncing some theologian or other as not Roman Catholic, or excommunicating. He is fundamentally pope when

[18] J. M. Cameron, *Images of Authority* (New Haven, Conn.: Yale University Press, 1966) xi, 2, 4–6.
[19] This view of authority, which underlies the entirety of this consideration, has been best expressed by Richard Flathman, *The Practice of Political Authority* (Chicago: University of Chicago Press, 1980).

he is celebrating the Eucharist and proclaiming the Word. If authority in the Church were fundamentally juridical, the Scriptures would have been incomplete until the promulgation of the Code of Canon Law in 1917. Faith is not a set of dogmatic statements, but the lived belief of the Church as evidenced in its whole life, especially its worship and works of mercy and charity. Christian morality is not a code of commandments, but the life of the Church community and the lives of the individual members as expressive of gospel values.

There are a number of problems with taking the juridical as paradigmatic for Church authority. First of all, the juridical focuses on the bottom-line requirements of authority: what are the minimal requirements of justice, the fundamental rights and obligations of the various members of the Church? Authority in the Church does and should encompass these minimal requirements, but more is asked of Christians in community, that is, the works of charity and mercy which cannot be legally prescribed or enforced. Laws can protect, but never generate life in the Spirit, the source of such works. Secondly, the juridical is inevitably abstract. It concentrates on the teaching of the Church, for instance, as a code or message understood in terms of the right of Church officials to teach and obligations of Church members to obey. What the people actually hear and heed is outside its ken. Finally, the juridical tends to be formal in its viewpoint. Thus, it concerns itself with procedural proprieties and questions of boundaries (who belongs and who doesn't). Religious authority, however, is about ends and not techniques, about the union of people with God and not their separation from other people. Only the celebration of the Eucharist and the proclamation of the Word can authentically express the purposes of the Church and its union with God. For this reason, Church authority is fundamentally sacramental.[20]

There is an important methodological point for this study in the assertion that authority in the Church is sacramental. Sacraments are symbolic actions which render the grace of God efficacious. As symbolic actions, they involve the words and gestures of human beings in community. Outside of time and apart from human factors, sacraments cannot exist. While the grace sacraments mediate means that more than the historical is involved, human history is the medium in which sacraments occur. Negatively, this sacramental character implies that there is no timeless essence

---

[20] The present pontiff has emphasized in a lecture he gave as archbishop of Cracow the significance of preaching the word for the office of bishop: Karol Wojtyla, "Bishops as Servants of the Faith," *Irish Theological Quarterly* 43 (1976) 260–73; that religious authority involves preaching the word and celebrating sacrament (among other things), cf. Buckley.

of Church authority which can be ontologically displayed. This does not mean that there is no "nature" of ecclesiastical authority. Rather, it means that the characteristics of Church authority can only be discovered in history. The story of the gospel and its interpretation in the tradition of the Church is the key to knowing what Church authority, as specifically Christian, is.

Conclusion

In conclusion, it might be helpful to lay bare several theses about authority which have been implicit in our critiques of alternative views and analyses.

(1) Authority makes possible the interchanges that bind a community together and enables the community to determine its identity; it is to that community what freedom is to the individual.[21] It is grounded in the authoritative, that set of norms and values the community holds or desires to hold.[22] The relationship between authority and the authoritative is analogous to that between freedom and character in the individual person.[23]

(2) Authority is a quality of human interaction with other persons and objects in community. It is the obligatory character of some rules of procedure implicit in those interactions. Some rules not only indicate how *x* is to be done, but also stipulate that *x* is better done than *y*. For instance, in learning a language, we learn not merely the grammar of the language, but the etiquette of preferring some ways of speaking ("I am not going to eat my dessert") to others ("I ain't going to eat that slop"); or, in learning to eat, we learn not only how to use a knife and fork, but also that eating that way is better than eating with our hands.[24]

(3) Synchronically, authority is a matter of a tension/balance between[25] the authority of equals related to one another for an event (liminality

---

[21] Buckley.

[22] Flathman.

[23] Buckley.

[24] Flathman.

[25] The words *tension/balance* here are not meant to convey a perfect equilibrium, only that, depending on the characteristics of the community, liminal and structural elements will be present as appropriate. Deborah Tannen in her book, *You Just Don't Understand* (N.Y.: William Morrow, 1990), observes on pages 24–25 that her husband engaged the world "as an individual in a hierarchical social order in which he was either one-up or one-down. In this world, conversations are negotiations in which people try to achieve and maintain the upper hand if they can, and protect themselves from others' attempts to put them down and push them around." On page 25 she observes that she by contrast approached the world

grounded in nature) and the authority of unequals arranged hierarchically (structure grounded in culture).[26] Diachronically, authority is a matter of tension/balance between what is given as plausible in the tradition and what possible alternatives to the given are deemed desirable as tradition questions itself in each succeeding historical moment.[27]

(4) The facts that given interpretations are essentially plausible rather than definitive and that the tradition is essentially open-ended mean that the authoritative is both the standard by which authority is evaluated and itself able to be called into question (at least in its particulars). Hence, dissent is a requirement lest the above tension/balances be irretrievably drawn in the direction of the structural and the plausible.[28] It is dissent which insures for authority its moral dimension, guaranteeing the possibility that we will be able to distinguish the good person from the good citizen, soldier, bureaucrat, etc.[29]

(5) Since human history is a history not only of grace and salvation, but also of sin and damnation, and often of the preferment of sin to grace, authority needs to be carefully and continually distinguished from authoritarianism. Just as coercion and inhibition are inimical to freedom, authoritarianism and ideology are the polar opposites of authority and its legitimation.

(6) Authority in the Church is sacramental as well as juridical, and it is the sacramental dimension which gives meaning to the juridical. This implies that, in the aforementioned tensions/balances, the true Church of Jesus Christ will prefer the liminal over the structural and the eschatologi-

---

"as an individual in a network of connections. In this world, conversations are negotiations for closeness in which people try to seek and give confirmation and support, and to reach consensus. They try to protect themselves from others' attempts to push them away." Tannen's book analyzes the different patterns in which men and women speak, and her analysis supports a conclusion (mine, not hers) that feminine speech contains more characteristics of liminality while masculine talk has more characteristics of structure. Thus, we could expect groups composed solely of men or women to combine liminal and structural elements differently.

[26] This concept is an application to authority of the work of Victor Turner, *The Ritual Process* (Ithaca, N.Y.: Cornell University Press, 1977).

[27] Cf. Paul Ricoeur, "Ideology and Utopia as Cultural Imagination," *Being Human in a Technological Age,* eds. D. M. Borchert and D. Stuart (Athens: Ohio University Press, 1979) 107–25.

[28] Flathman has insisted on the necessity of dissent for the proper exercise of authority although he has argued his position in another manner.

[29] Schaar, *Escape From Authority,* 299–300.

cal to the "traditional." Finally, the "essence of Christian authority" is accessible only through a study of how it has evolved historically.

In the remaining chapters of this book, these six theses will be argued and explicated. The theses are adumbrated here to give the reader a sense of the directions in which the book is moving.

CHAPTER 3

What Is Authority?

The General Notion of Authority

The central purpose of this chapter will be to answer the question: What is authority? In view of the previous chapter, every effort will be made to avoid an analysis which discusses authority as the property of a person or thing. Rather, authority needs to be analyzed as a social reality—and, hence, needs to be seen from the perspective of a postmodernist theology.[1] From this perspective authority is a practice, an interaction that binds the author and the recipient together in the context of what the community holds in common and what the traditions of the community have bequeathed to its present members.

Briefly, authority is what enables a community to be bound together in all its interactions. In the life of a community, authority plays a role that is analogous to the role freedom plays in the life of an individual. Authority makes it possible for a community to determine what it is and to have a sense of purpose. Without it, human beings become a horde of animals in competition with one another for the satisfaction of urges. Authority, then, functions at the heart of our living together.

---

[1] Postmodernism here refers to theoretical endeavors which are based on the philosophical writings of the later Wittgenstein and the later Heidegger. For both these thinkers, knowledge is a matter of interpretation and not of representation. Knowledge consists in a conversation with other people and physical reality. In general, both Wittgenstein and Heidegger eschew the modern philosophic quest after foundations, things in themselves (the attainment of an objectivity independent of our perspective on them), and universal characteristics of a transcendental subject. All human knowing is historical, inclusive of the particular as well as the universal, and radically finite.

Why do we have authority? The first answer is that it provides us with unity of action in community. Any experience of life together teaches us that there are several roads to any particular end we wish to achieve. Even our most enlightened and least egotistical peers often disagree over policy. One says this is the way to go; another proposes an alternative. If we were left to ourselves as individuals, one decision would cancel out or retard another so that, in the sweep of time, all decisions would be canceled out by one another or have outcomes which were neither foreseen nor desired by the individual decision-makers. Given the pluralism of possible ways to proceed, we require authority to determine that the community go in one direction and not another. Otherwise, it would be paralyzed in the face of too many directions to pursue. In short, authority functions as the prudence of a society in its collective action.

A second answer to the question, "Why have authority?" is friendship—in a sense familiar to the way in which Aristotle saw friendship as the goal of his fellow Greeks' living together in the *polis*. Individual freedom is not merely freedom from external and internal coercion; it is also realization in life. Freedom aims not at isolation, but at union. This union is achieved when people come to mutual understanding and actualization in the process of communicating with and revealing themselves to one another. The free individual attains liberty in its fullest form in a society where all can speak openly of their most cherished values and ideals without defenses or suspicion. Freedom flourishes in societies where dreams and meanings are shared and grow to maturity. Authority, then, promotes the kinds of community in which people can live together in the trust and confidence that beget friendship. In the give and take of human living together, authority enables us to work out our destiny as truly free human beings, that is, as persons who are free together.

Authority obviously bears an intimate relationship to freedom. Freedom can never be adequately viewed as simply independence from others. Independence is certainly one of the great gifts of freedom, but the freedom of one individual needs to be brought to its fulfillment by another's. Otherwise, the ideal free society would be a jungle. One of the first functions of authority is to set limits on the independence of the individual members of the group. But that is not all. Authority also makes possible the doing of things together that would not be feasible if we all were simply isolated individuals. For instance, one could hardly imagine the mobility that characterizes life today if each and every individual had to build his or her means of transportation.

The limitations authority imposes on free individuals bear closer attention. The modes in which authority is exercised are the products of human innovation. Such innovation, however, is not simply an individual affair. Innovation presumes style—what people generally consider creative and not destructive. On the basis of style, a shared reality, we construct some kinds of authority and not others. Once authority is in place, it provides a context in which individuals can participate and thus obtain the goods not possible in isolation and be independent as human persons, and not as rapacious animals. Authority lays down the rules of the game for the enhancement of participation and independence. Any practice of authority must function so that it is understood, organized, and conducted such that it maximizes its compatibility with and contribution to the agency of all.

The core assertion of this chapter is that authority is a human practice. But what is meant by "human practice"? Playing baseball, singing jingles, and making promises are human practices. So are giving orders, assigning tasks to be done, and determining who will receive what. Human practices are not acts done by individuals in isolation from one another even though, as the previous chapter argued, traditional analyses of authority have tended to conceive them so. Human practices are interactions that link individuals together and establish the relationship that constitutes human sociability. In the giving of an order two people are tied together in that one assumes the obligation to carry out the order (usually ascribing superior wisdom to the other) and the other rests assured that what needs to be done will be done (and knows that he or she doesn't have to do everything himself or herself). Not only are human practices not isolating actions, but they are social realities and historical creations as well. Playing baseball is a practice performed quite commonly in the United States and in a handful of nations around the world, but in the majority of countries around the world today it is virtually unknown. And playing baseball does have its own peculiar history. Just compare batting averages in the two major leagues over the first forty years of this century to those in more recent years, before and after pitchers developed and commonly used the slider and other assorted pitches and batters started concentrating on hitting home runs.

Another word besides practice for describing authority is competence. Competence brings out an important feature of authority. We consider people competent for one of two reasons: either they are endowed with certain personal qualities that are held in high esteem, or they have received their ability to act through a particular delegation or a pattern of doing so in the society. Competencies are, in the first sense, social excellences. One excellence held in high esteem since the time of Jesus is humility. Christianity is hardly imaginable without it. Nor are the secularized societies of the West without generalized reverence for humility. We all prefer the home run hitter who says, "Aw shucks, I just got good wood on the ball," to the one who tells us how many hours he has spent perfecting his batting stroke.[2] Competence also can be delegated. God or the people, custom and law, have dictated over the centuries that some persons and not others should be able to give orders and create social realities, for example, declare a couple married.

Our first and primal encounter with the notion of authority is learning a language. There we engage in a prolonged and complex process of aping the adult world and by trial and error, gradually attaining the mutuality with others that speaking a language makes possible. We learn that some ways of saying things are correct and others are not. Most of this learning is by osmosis. But even explicit instructions are by and large taken as gospel truth. It is in learning language that we first acquire the notion that some people are authorities because they exhibit certain skills or because they have been granted a role such as parenting.

Any overview of authority requires one final consideration for completeness. Each particular instance of authority is imperfect. This means not simply that each exercise of authority is finite, but that it contains what Christians call sinful elements. From experience, we have learned to beware of the ministrations of any teacher, no matter how wise and gracious. Teachers, while they may be initially helpful, can and often do become corrupt and corrupting in the end. Any knowledge of history further tells us that even the most impressive instances of public authority have discouraged and deflected participation of whole categories of people, suppressed arguments and modes of action that were perfectly well grounded, imposed rules that served the narrow interests of the ruling elite, and employed threats and coercion against innocent and exemplary citizens. Any realistic consideration of authority needs to take this underside of the practice of authority into account.[3]

---

[2] Alasdair MacIntyre observes in *After Virtue* that humility is conspicuous by its absence from all the lists of virtues in the writings of ancient pagan writers. The fact that we consider it a virtue is a distinctive contribution of Christian tradition to Western culture.

[3] The principal influence in this section is Michael Buckley, "Authority," *Agora* (Autumn 1968); I have also made use of Richard Flathman, *The Practice of Political Authority* (Chicago: University of Chicago Press, 1980); Carl Friedrich, *Tradition and Authority* (London: Pall Mall, 1972); Nicholas Lash, *Voices of Authority* (Shepherdstown: Patmos, 1976); John Schaar, "Reflections on Authority," *New American Review* (VIII); Yves Simon, *A General Theory of Authority* (Notre Dame: Notre Dame University Press, 1962); and Joseph Vining, *The Authoritative and the Authoritarian* (Chicago: University of Chicago Press, 1986).

Authority as a Practice

One author has defined a practice as a set of considerations, manners, uses, observances, customs, standards, canons, maxims, principles, rules, and offices specifying useful procedures or denoting obligations and duties which relate to human actions or utterances.[4] A few examples here would undoubtedly help. A football coach tells the quarterback to throw a screen pass in the left flat to the fullback. A judge hands down a verdict in favor of the plaintiff. A mother tells her child to wash his hands before supper. A teacher makes *Pride and Prejudice* the reading assignment for the next class. Sending in a play, rendering a verdict, ordering a child, and giving homework are all practices of authority in our society. To add "of authority" to "practices" implies that one person interacts with one or more other persons in such a way that the other(s) is linked to the first by an obligation assumed. The quarterback, if he calls a run, violates the rules of the practice. The defendant, if she lays hold of what was in dispute, does the same. So also the child who continues playing or the student who appears in the next class without having read Jane Austen. The manifold number of ways in which authority can be exercised includes starting actions which others complete, gaining assent, and making recommendations not safely ignored because they are usually right. In any case, authority is an interaction which binds together at least two persons, one who has assumed an obligation and another who is acknowledged as being able to act in the name of the group. This "acting in the name of" can have two sources: a highly regarded skill is displayed in the actor's behavior or the capacity to act has been delegated by the community.

Authority, then, is an attribute of human interaction among human agents and the objects which surround them. It is embedded in their social organizations. As such, practices of authority do change from one epoch to another, are done differently in various societies, and are altered to suit the occasion. Teaching is a practice of authority. But that authority is exercised quite differently depending on whether one lectures, leads a discussion, or conducts a Socratic dialogue. Furthermore, teaching in the First World, where library collections are substantial and textbooks readily accessible, is different from teaching in the Third World, where books are neither readily available nor easily affordable. Finally, one would have to search widely today for the kind of instruction that was taken for granted in much of the ancient world: learning to write and to be morally wise through slavish copying of moral maxims dictated by the teacher.

---

[4] Flathman, the central influence on this section and the two following.

What is the difference between a mere practice and a practice of authority? Playing chess is a practice. Teaching another to play chess makes a chess player an authority. On occasion being a chess master involves authority insofar as one plays chess so well that others are compelled to acknowledge one as a model for the practice. In both these latter two cases, at least one other person is placed under an obligation to do as he or she is told or as the chess master does if he or she wants to learn to play chess and to play well. Also, in each of these cases, someone is acknowledged as being able to act in the name of the group, the group being those who know how to play or those who play chess masterfully. It so happens that in both of these examples the relationship moves toward equality: one seeks to learn or play as well as the teacher or master. Some exercises of authority, however, involve structural inequalities between the person obliged and the one in whose name one is acting. Without violence prisoners cannot gain equality with the warden, nor citizens with the head of state unless they succeed to that high office.

Authority is a widespread phenomenon in our communities. Often it is only implicitly recognized and ranges along a continuum from the personal and intimate to the structural and abstract. If we are to grasp what authority is, we need to focus our attention not only on heads of state, teachers, and masters of skills, but also on the citizenry, students, and the imitators who are placed under obligation.

Another way of distinguishing between human practices in general and practices of authority is that the latter are always perceived as *the* way of doing things. There are many ways of being a small forward in basketball, but Larry Bird has set the standard for the time being and, in time, someone else will set another. There are numerous imaginable ways of preventing legislation from coming to pass, but bottling the proposed law up in committee, filibusters, and presidential veto are the ways it is done in the United States of America. In either kind of case, authority is a practice conceived as *the* way of practicing, whether *the* refers to what is standard, or customary, or legal. In other words, authority is a practice which is normative, whether the practice is so by embodying or being in a formal way designated the norm. The sources of *the* quality can be natural endowment, special knowledge, immemorial custom, a constitution, or a law—to specify only those which are usually mentioned.

The Grammar of Authority as a Practice

All human practices are rule-governed behavior. The rules in question may be explicit or at least able to be made so, but are often, and to a certain extent are always, implicit and known only tacitly. This obtains whether we are playing a game, passing legislation, speaking a language, or forming a friendship. In the first three instances, we find explicit rules in a rule book, a legal code, or a book of grammar. Additionally, there are implicit or tacit rules which specify what can and cannot be done if the practice is to be done properly. In baseball, for example, the rule book explicitly stipulates what is a strike, what is a ball, and how many of each the batter and pitcher are allowed. But no rule book tells the pitcher that it is wise to throw an 0 and 2 pitch out of the strike zone, or a batter to hit a 2 and 0 pitch only when it is the pitch he is looking for. It is these tacit rules (what Wittgenstein called "depth grammar" as opposed to surface grammar that can be and often is codified) that give to baseball its style. Knowing the depth grammar of baseball enables player and spectator alike to distinguish between just playing the game and playing well. In the final example above, friendship, learning the depth grammar is crucial; all the books of etiquette in the world will not help us make friends if we have not mastered the tacit rules of the practice. Depth grammar varies from place to place, and from time to time. Making friends in the United States is a casual and relatively easy matter. In France, moving from "vous" to "tu" is more arduous and lengthy; it also results in a more complex and demanding relationship. Yet making friends in either the U.S. or France today is vastly different from what it was in Aristotle's Athens where the bulk of the population were excluded from consideration because they were foreigners, slaves, or women.

For practices of authority, the distinction between surface and depth grammar looms large. Personal and intimate practices of authority depend almost exclusively on tacit rules, while structural and abstract practices depend on explicit rules for their being and tacit rules for their well-being. In the latter cases, following the rules is equivalent to assuming roles, occupying statuses, and adhering to norms. In either set of cases, participating in the practices includes thinking and acting within the limits thereof; that is, within the constraints of the rules and guidelines that the rules establish such that certain modes of thought and action are permitted, encouraged, or required and others are tolerated, discouraged, or even prohibited. In football, for instance, the rule book stipulates that a team scores a field goal when a member of the team either place kicks or drop-kicks the ball from behind the line of scrimmage through the uprights and above the crossbar. Until thirty years ago, it had not occurred to most coaches or players that both accuracy and distance could be improved if the ball were kicked soccer style. Kicking soccer style does have its rules, but they are more likely to be displayed in good field goal kicking than in something written down.

In football the rule book states the explicit rules or surface grammar while the depth grammar is tacitly embodied in the performance of the outstanding players. Since the rules involved in practices of authority involve both surface and depth grammar, such practices display a certain indeterminacy. Any community tolerates tacitly only some styles for being a charismatic figure, but passes explicit laws governing the exercise of offices and admits only some ways of performing in office well. Just as the laws of the land can be changed, so too the depth grammar in question evolves over time and according to circumstances.

The rules inherent in any practice of authority are interactive. That is, the rules empower one person to act in the name of the community and require others to assume an obligation. The chess master plays chess in a manner that the community deems playing it well, and the aspirant has to model his or her play on that of the master if he or she is to learn the game properly. Likewise the coach, acting in the name of the whole team, sends in the play and the quarterback is obliged to call that play unless he wants to sit on the bench, that is, not participate in the practice.

Bedrock and Belief

The rules of a practice of authority are themselves the reasons for keeping them. They constitute the bedrock of the practice, bedrock here meaning the place where arguments end, not because we are absolutely certain, but because we agree that it makes no sense to ask further questions. The rules are equivalent to what people consider "natural" about the practice. They function either as the way things are or as the way they ought to be (and often as both) at this particular time and in this particular place. Rules, we have already noted, have the character of indeterminacy. Rules in rule books are rewritten. So are tacit rules. Six-foot-nine-inch guards come along and change the way professional basketball is played. We need, however, to note the constrained pace in which such change usually occurs. Some, not all, the rules are rewritten. Basketball is still recognizably the same game as it was before the arrival of Magic Johnson. The bedrock, while socially and historically constituted, does possess a relative fixity. This qualified indeterminacy of the rules, especially at the level of depth grammar, has another aspect. Exercises of authority are better viewed in the comparative and not the superlative mode. The rules generally stipulate not that x is the best course of action in an absolute fashion, but that x is better done than its alternative y. At the present time, the community either agrees on the desirability of doing x or can conceive of no better alternative to x. Thus, all practices and exercises of authority are finite in character. They can and may very well be improved upon. But, as the collective wisdom of the community in the here-and-now and over the ages, the rules are not easily or readily discarded.

Such rules, which are central to our understanding of authority, are a comparatively formal reality. For some human practices, the community authorizes certain ways of performing the practice as the way things are done, or done well. The rules always function against the background of some sort of institutionalized arrangement. Some of these arrangements are quite formal, that is, structured, and grant position in a hierarchy; others are informal, that is, liminal, and describe the excellences esteemed by the group.

In either event, practices of authority depend on three beliefs. First, conformity with established rules is the criterion by which proposed rules are properly judged. In other words, the established rules are bedrock. The use of *conformity* here might raise some hackles. But we need to notice that rarely does anyone object to conforming with a good and noble cause. In fact, conformity to rules for authority is so widespread in our complex societies that we scarcely notice it. When conformity as such does come to our attention, and when people cry out against it, we are usually dealing with conformity to the trivial; it is possible for rules to lose their sense as circumstances change. Secondly, these and not those rules are the established rules. Basketball at the Olympics is played differently from the way it is played in the National Basketball Association. But if the game is to be played at all, it needs to be played according to one set of rules and not the other. Thirdly, this and not that interpretation of the rules is the correct one. Stating the rules and interpreting them are not two discrete realities. Homeric warriors may strike us as exceptionally arrogant. We might also be puzzled that Homer uses the word *virtue* for what we call athletic abilities, for example, the capacity to run swiftly. Within the text, from the perspective of the interaction of the characters with one another, it makes no sense to question the correctness of the poet's view. We can, however, raise critical questions because of our cultural separation from the Homeric world. But within our own culture we need to acknowledge that almost all our human practices are accompanied by the belief that rules of procedure exist, and that the standard interpretations of those rules are correct ones.

Rule-Following: Ends and Means

Human rule-following is not an aimless undertaking. All the rules involved in practices of authority require considerations of purpose, desirability, and ends. But we want to emphasize that these considerations are *internal* to framing, promulgating, identifying, and being guided by rules. The meaning of *internal* here can be elaborated in terms of two contrasts.

First, the purposes of authoritative rules are internal to the rules in the sense that they are implicit in the practice itself. For instance, professional athletes are paid performers, yet members of championship teams regularly report that the monetary rewards seldom inspire the sacrifices necessary for winning it all. Money, the kudos of the crowd, meetings with the president at the White House are all extrinsic goods. The good internal to the practice is playing the game as close to perfection as is humanly possible such that winning a championship becomes more likely and, for members of one team, actual. Secondly, the word *internal* implies that the ends which are significant in analyzing any practice of authority are shared among the participants. People may enter into a practice of authority for manifold personal reasons. They imagine and desire some outcome or satisfaction. But it is the historically determined and now commonly shared purposes of the practices which dictate whether an exercise of authority is valid or not, licit or not. Thus, if the president of the United States might attempt to promulgate a law by presidential decree (and outside any powers already granted by Congress), and even if he does so for the noblest of motives, the United States does not have a new law. If he follows the appropriate procedures by proposing the measure to Congress and having it passed by both houses, and does so for the most venal of motives, the United States has a new law.

Sometimes these ends or purposes are final and sometimes they are instrumental. Final ends have to do with what the community considers distinctively human about the practice in question. Charismatic figures can exercise extensive authority if they display the virtues which are most highly esteemed in society. Officials in a hierarchy exercise authority in terms of either what is explicitly stated in the legislation according power in a particular instance or of what is regarded as canonical or classical in the community. For example, the performance of American presidents is often judged with the guidance of foundational documents like the Declaration of Independence and the Constitution along with speeches of highly regarded past presidents. The performances of past presidents also serve as models. Acting in accord with the law, which reflects basic beliefs about the human, is a bottom line criterion. Instrumental means have to do with the links which obtain between a human practice and objects in the world. For example, the conduct of the American presidency today is quite different from that of the nineteenth century, given the development of air travel. While both final and instrumental means are internal to practices of authority, the two are inextricably intertwined and mutually dependent. It is feckless to project and promise final values unless we control the means to them and pointless to labor for the procurement of instrumental values unless these issue in final ones. People who do the former are utopian dreamers; people who do the latter are pedestrian bureaucrats. In neither case are they authorities in the proper sense!

Communication and Authority

Exercises of authority involve communication between at least two persons. Usually the communication is verbal, but it may be otherwise; for instance in certain circumstances one can order by pointing. The communications are transactions between the parties involved and follow certain laws of language. First, these communications, like all language and human behavior, are open-ended within limits. Neither the authority figure nor the assumer of the obligation has the last word. For the person called to obey, not just anything counts as a fulfillment of what has been commanded. Communities do place limits on possible outcomes; they also revise those limits from time to time. Likewise the one giving the order is required to articulate the command in terms of either the ability he or she displays or the delegation received. Secondly, communications are publicly shared realities. They depend on agreements which are tacitly known throughout most of the community. For this reason authority is characterized by an inherent mutuality. A practice of authority is not present when a person issues a command to no one, nor when the person commanded assumes no public responsibility for what is said ("I was just carrying out orders"). Moreover, the person carrying out the order does so not merely as an individual, but as member of the group. He or she expects at least one other person, usually the one who gave the order, to agree that a certain behavior counts as fulfilling the command. In short, the practice of authority as a communication requires appropriate attitudes and action from all the parties involved.

We experience both these features of communication—its open-endedness within limits and its public, shared character—when we pick up a book and read it. The books we really treasure make sense to us because of what we possess in common with the author as a potential member of our own community. People can read Jane Austen with much profit and enjoyment without ever knowing anything about the author as an individual. It is on the basis of a shared, rule-governed practice—reading—that we communicate with her. Furthermore, in reading a book we attend directly to what the author says, what he or she means. Ordinary, and intelligent, readers do not look first for the venality, duplicity, temper, class-bias, ambition or illness the text displays. Critical questioning arises in the context of an overall trust that unites us to the author as another person sharing in certain human skills. Yet when we read a book, there is a certain to-and-fro, conversational character about our interpretation. We are engaged in a process of retrieval. We project a meaning and allow that meaning to be amplified or corrected through further reading. Throughout the whole process, our aim is not to reconstruct what an author meant in the past, but to gain an understanding of what the text can mean for us in the present. While we are determining what the meaning of the text is, we are also determining whether that meaning will be meaning for us. This consideration of reading as a conversation reveals that (1) the publicly shared character of authoritative communications requires mutuality and trust which precede and ground critical inquiry, and (2) that its open-ended within-limits aspect makes possible a situation in which participants in any practice of authority are both dependent upon the practice as a given and co-creators of the practice in its evolution.

Books from the past are important because of the wisdom they contain. We read them not to know the mind of an author lurking behind the text, but to know ourselves better, to take possession of ourselves historically. Reading a text enables us to know whence we came and where we are. Those works we call classics embody the past which has made us. We continue to read them because they never cease to speak to us. What they have to say is only partially realized in past interpretations which have left much unsaid. To speak that unsaid is the task of present interpretation.[5]

Similarly, when an authoritative communication imposes an obligation on someone, it does so in such a way that the mutuality of the interaction is preserved as well as the agency of the person who assumes the obligation. To attribute obligation is to attribute agency. Neither coercion nor manipulation are consonant with the practice of authority in normal circumstances. Resorting to force is justified only where command, decision, recommendation, and persuasion have failed. Authentic authority enhances individual freedom. In fact, a general principle for evaluating authoritative acts involving mature and decent actors, is that authority and voluntary assent mutually enrich each other.

Authority and Responsibility

It follows from all the above that a person who gives an order is appropriately expected to be caring and responsible. A simply impersonal authority does not exist. Only what can speak to us can exercise authority over us; otherwise issues of obedience or disobedience do not arise. One

---

[5] Obviously, I am here making use of Gadamer's model of understanding. Cf. Hans-Georg Gadamer, *Truth and Method,* 2nd, rev. ed. with a translation revised by Joel Weinsheimer and Donald Marshall (N.Y.: Crossroad, 1989).

assumes that the authoritative voice means what it says, cares about what it asks another to do, believes in what it requests others to believe. A figure who is cold, distant, uncaring, and irresponsible about the consequences of commands significantly diminishes his or her real authority. The best authority figures make us feel like insiders to the decision-making process. They are open, speak their minds out loud, reveal their purposes, and do not hold things back.

Nor, on this understanding of authority, does the person who assumes an obligation become a merely passive recipient. All members of any community contribute to the formation of its rules and can initiate plans and actions as new circumstances arise. Recipients of a command must be regarded as agents, i.e., as persons who engage in self-actuated, intentional, purposive, and rational behavior. It is considered perverse in most cases if the person in authority does not allow for initiative in carrying out an order. Thus, authority is often best analyzed by attending not to what the authority figures say, but to what the recipients of an order hear. If what is said is not regularly heard and heeded, it is difficult to argue that we have an instance of authority. Insofar as recipients continue to pay attention to orders, the latter continue to embody authority. They obey because they agree with the order itself or the overall context in which it is given. A good way to know the genuine (and not feigned) mind of most people is to pay attention to the kinds of orders they carry out, especially the ones where they do so with verve and enthusiasm.

In every instance, a practice of authority is vicarious. From a religious perspective, it is exercised "under God"; from a political perspective, it derives from the community as a whole. Authority is never at the disposal of either the giver or the receiver of a command. People who use authority in their own self-interest are always abusing their power and risk losing it altogether; likewise, nor are those who pander to their followers or subjects. True authority is self-effacing. It urges both parties to the transaction towards selfless and generous living. Since authority ought to be understood as always under God and generally from the people, human authorities are never total or absolute. Yet recipients of commands reasonably do regard the authority of the giver as a weighty reason (the basis of a *prima facie* obligation) for doing what is required, though they should not accord conclusive weight to such an authority. All human authorities are situated in an area between absolute certitudes and methodical doubting.[6]

[6] Besides Flathman and Friedrich, Lash, Schaar, and Vining (who have already been noted), I have made use of Robert Bierstadt, "The Problem of Authority," *Freedom and Control in Modern Society,* eds. Morroe Berger, Theodore Abel, and Charles Paye (N.Y.: Octagon Books, 1964); J. M. Cameron, *Images of Authority*

Summary

Authority, then, is a human, that is, socially shared and historically produced practice. In the practice, an obligation is laid on one party while another party is enabled to speak and/or act in the name of the community. Practices of authority are distinguished from other human practices in that the rules inherent in the practices are themselves the reasons for keeping the rules because these rules are stipulated in laws, embedded in custom, or constitute the bedrock whereby the community has its life. The transactions or communications between the parties who participate in a practice of authority both respect the agency of the parties and enhance their capacities for fuller living.

Authority Synchronically Considered

In the first chapter we observed that human communities are actually two realities in dialectical relationship. On the one hand, people relate to one another liminally, as a communion of equals. Community from this perspective is an event happening here and now where personal qualities are central. The members stress spontaneity and keeping in touch with themselves as bonded to nature. Organization at this level is open-ended, suited to particular purposes, and characterized by communication which is highly metaphorical and affective. Communities, however, are also something else since people relate to each other also structurally, as a society of unequals. Community from this other perspective is a differentiated and hierarchical system. The members stress social obligations and place limits on expressions of spontaneity to mobilize group resources for group goals. Structured organization results from clearly articulated thought and sustained will. In this structural perspective, people speak in the cognitive mode, think atomistically (breaking complex tasks into the simplest elements), and are concerned about boundaries. Without liminality, community is lifeless; without structure, it cannot perdure.[7]

Because community is two distinguishable realities, authority takes two quite different forms, even though most of our recognizable authori-

---

(New Haven: Yale University Press, 1966); Iredell Jenkins, "Authority: Its Nature and Locus," *Authority: A Philosophical Analysis,* ed. R. Baine Harris (Athens, Ala.: University of Alabama Press, 1976); William Meissner, *The Assault on Authority* (Maryknoll: Orbis, 1971); John Wild, "Authority," *Authority,* ed. Frederick Adelman (The Hague: Martinus Nijhoff, 1974).

[7] Victor Turner, *The Ritual Process: Structure and Anti-Structure* (Ithaca, N.Y.: University of Cornell Press, 1977) and Ph. G. Herbst, *Alternatives to Hierarchies* (Leiden: Martinus Nijhoff, 1976).

ties display both forms in their actual performance. We need to distinguish between *an* authority, which is also called charismatic and sometimes epistemic authority, and *in* authority, which is also called official or deontic. The life of the party is *an* authority, while the quintessential bureaucrat relies on *in* authority. Founders of communities are invariably examples of *an* authority. The administrators who succeed them in leadership function *in* authority. Teachers, heads of government, and managers of enterprise depend on *in* authority for their positions, but must display *an* authority if they are to act well in their capacities.

An authorities are persons, texts, and documents whose authority consists in the possession of some attribute widely esteemed in society. We admire them for the intellectual, moral, or artistic abilities they display (or all three at once). This wisdom, character, and originality are admired because *an* authorities embody in their actions the broadly esteemed excellences of the group, the valued types of skills. This esteem and valuation may vary according to the circumstances. On the playing field physical courage commands much respect. When the dam has just burst, prudent retreat is called for. In the Old Testament, cunning and trickery are held in high esteem even where parents are involved and significant matters are at stake. In industrialized societies today such chicanery plays a more restricted role. *An* authority is accorded in terms of a certain "more or less." Those virtues which command the greatest respect in any group are always the sources of the greatest *an* authority. Being able to draw up a game plan that maximizes the strength of the team and exploits the weakness of the opposition is more important to good football coaching than giving inspirational pre-game or half-time talks. In general, being honest, generous, and open-minded are better regarded than being clean or having a good memory. *An* authority can come and go. It may possess authority for one group and not another, or for one epoch and not another. And even in the same group according to different circumstances, it may or may not be authoritative. It is part of the nature of *an* authority that it is of the moment. It is inherently occasional even though an instance of *an* authority may recall some previous instances and be reinforced thereby.

In contrast, the temporality of *in* authority differs from that of *an* authority. For *in* authority each moment comes out of the past and is being thrust into the future. *In* authority temporally involves sequence and, therefore, permanence. It also involves systems of rules and institutions, the latter often of a legal nature. These systems of rules create offices which enable their occupants to give orders by right rather than by skill or virtue. Strictly speaking, it is the office and not the occupant which possesses authority. Groups freely form themselves into permanent associations in which they designate that specific tasks will be carried out only by some, namely the designated officials to whom the group delegates the power to act in the name of and for the good of the group. These officials are expected to harmonize and orchestrate the efforts of the members into a unity. Since delegation is always in some sense specific, at least in terms of the goods internal to the practice, official power is always limited. This specificity and concomitant limitation of power constitute our principal criteria for evaluating the use and abuse of *in* authority.

Authority to give official commands generally requires institutional justification. That is, people who are confronted by an exercise of *in* authority do not look to the merits of the order given but to the issues of whether the official has been properly designated and whether the command is given within the confines of the delegation. For *in* authority, the context for evaluation is in all cases the rules creating the office and its scope; what the community believes and values is relevant to evaluation only in some instances. Moreover, while *an* authority leans on custom, *in* authority relies on law. Laws are crucial if groups are to move from savagery to civilization. Laws constitute the prudent conclusions that the group has drawn from the past and its forethought for facing the future responsibly.

This penchant for judging the actions of officials on the basis of their legality and not the merits of the command has, of course, led to numerous abuses of *in* authority. The solution to this historically well-documented problem, however, does not lie either in an anarchy which repudiates all institutional authority or in an ethics of suspicion which decrees that obedience should be given only when the merits of the case are demonstrated. The solution to this pattern of abuse lies in our remembering that the permanence of *in* authority is temporal. Its exercise must necessarily display responsible agency on the part of both superior and subject. We can restate this last assertion in the form of a principle: wherever superiors and subjects are showing initiative in their commanding and obedience, enabling more and more members of the group to participate in the practice and fostering individual differences, the more likely it is that the commands given and orders carried out accord with the beliefs and values of the community. For authority functions in community for the enhancement of freedom in the members.

Where the system of rules becomes completely depersonalized, it can no longer be maintained that we have an instance of *in* authority. *In* authority must not only permit but encourage the fullness of personality in the members of the community.[8] Moreover, though in industrialized socie-

---

[8] We need to note that this fullness of personality here is the realization in life that friends can achieve only in union with one another, and not what is called self-actualization in humanistic psychology.

ties law is the main prop for *in* authority, it can never be the exclusive guide. Law always requires the supplement of custom, especially those customs which embody what the community counts as humane.

In conclusion, it cannot be stated too strongly that almost all the examples of authority we know in our day-to-day lives involve both *an* and *in* authority. The distinction is largely notional, theoretical, and abstract. Considerations of concrete instances of *in* authority generally require some *an* authority norms. Exclusively *an* authority, though possible, is rare.[9]

Authority Diachronically Considered

Authority considered in the light of the temporal before and after is called *tradition*. Tradition may be defined as "a system of symbols which act to establish powerful, persuasive, and long-standing moods and motivations by formulating conceptions of the general order of existence and clothing those conceptions in such an aura of factuality or possibility that the moods and motivations are seen to be uniquely realistic or realizable."[10] This definition highlights the linguistic character of any tradition and how profoundly its language penetrates the communal psyche. The definition further emphasizes that authentic tradition never simply counsels the mere repetition of the past but looms as a bulwark against arbitrary excursions into the future. Thus, it simultaneously conserves and alters itself. Another helpful definition states that a tradition is a "coherent body of shared memories, images, ideas, and ideals which orient over time and space, linking past, present, and future into a meaningful whole and tying means and ends into a continuum beyond the narrowly pragmatic and expedient."[11] This definition brings out the fact that tradition informs the members of the community at the tacit level: it provides the presuppositions of what the members consider plausible or possible, and it is expressed in

---

[9] Besides Flathman, Friedrich, and Schaar, see Richard McGeorge, "The Nature and Function of Epistemic Authority," *Authority,* ed. Harris.

[10] This description of tradition is based on Paul Ricoeur, "Ideology and Utopia as Cultural Imagination," *Being Human in a Technological Age,* eds. D. M. Borchert and D. Stuart (Athens, Ala.: Ohio University Press, 1979) 107–76. In the essay Ricoeur distinguishes sharply between ideology which looks to the past and utopia which envisions a future. I am here contending that ideology and utopia in his terminology are two indistinguishable aspects of tradition. Ricoeur has expanded his ideas in his *Lectures on Ideology and Utopia,* ed. George H. Taylor (N.Y.: Columbia University Press, 1986).

[11] Schaar, "Reflections on Authority," 56. I have altered the words of Schaar slightly, combining two sentences into one.

their habits, customs, and laws. The definition also clarifies that tradition makes it possible for the community to have a history. Through tradition means and ends and moments of time are no longer disconnected atoms, but elements in a story which has a wholeness or meaning which can be narrated. A final definition that will prove helpful especially in articulating the authoritative character of tradition asserts that tradition is "a set of convictions and beliefs concerning community and behavior defining how rule is conducted and how the ruled behave toward their rulers, including electing and controlling them, i.e., the prevalent values and beliefs expressed in habits, customs, and norms."[12] A tradition is authoritative because it is mediated to us in the bedrock rules of certain practices. Further, a tradition is both passively received and actively assimilated. We are born, socialized, and mature within a tradition which we then are free to shape, at least in some of its particulars.

All three of these definitions share the same important assumption, namely that human existence is a being together with others in a world such that our humanity is primarily constituted by mutuality and historicity. Tradition is like the air we breathe. It claims us at birth and ushers us into the to-and-fro of history until death parts us from its grasp. We listen to the tradition by allowing others (people and texts principally) to enter our lives and moving out to these others in conversations about beliefs and values. None of this is meant to assert that individuality and freedom are illusions, only that they are conditioned realities through which we become aware of our peculiar insertion into the tradition (how our biographies are separable from the community's history) and of those beliefs and values for which we will die (how the moral exercise of individual liberty is not identical with communal expectations for public behavior).

The tradition provides us with our sense of what is right and proper and enables us in that light to leave some things unchanged, yet insist that other matters bear close scrutiny and/or must be altered. The truth of tradition is generally obvious and rarely argued, most often believed and only seldom proven. Its truth constitutes the basis for all rational discourse and reasoned decision-making in a given social milieu. While it always maintains a certain equilibrium, tradition is ever on the move in some of its constituent parts. Although change in the tradition frequently goes unperceived at the time, its movements become obvious to subsequent generations who then write histories within the tradition. Nor is tradition all of a piece. It is enfleshed in individuals each one of whose insertion into the

---

[12] Friedrich, 18. Again, I have altered Friedrich, reducing three sentences into one and generalizing what he says. Friedrich was defining a political tradition.

tradition is never of entirely the same cloth as any others. Individual members of the community agree with some people on certain beliefs and values, with other people on other aspects of the tradition. Moreover, traditions differ according to the shape of the community involved. Closed societies usually agree on almost all the fundamental values and beliefs; open societies are more pluralistic. Finally, tradition is found in people as they are—full of noble ideas, generous aspirations, magnificent desires but also plagued by prejudices, vices, and fears. Like the air we breathe, it is polluted.

Tradition is foundationally temporal. It has a past which can be narrated in chronicles which tell its story in a sequence of before and after. These chronicles give tradition its fixity. Tradition also has a future. It constructs scenarios which anticipate behaviors and institutions that better what has been. These scenarios provide tradition with both a sense of an ending and a certain indeterminacy. Tradition, finally, is embodied in the present. Here stories are told of selves acting in concert. These stories become human history when the tale is told neither as a mechanical succession of moments in time nor as a fantasy ungrounded in the present, but as a set of decisions made by people acting together in the face of the possibilities engendered by the past and the environment. Tradition does have its shadow side. It can become obtuse and see the past or future as undifferentiated from the present; history in such cases speaks of repeatable cycles. Tradition can become also abstract and see the moments in the chronicle or the scenarios as disconnected and random events. Or it can attempt to flee history and snatch altogether at the being of higher, angel-like powers. Archaism, abstraction, and spiritualism are the sins of tradition.

We have insisted that tradition, at least in its parts, is always in flux. Fidelity to tradition is ill conceived if we view it as repetition of the past. The understanding tradition makes possible is not reducible to confirmation of what we already know or a search for what is repeatable, unchanging, and certain within it. The discipline tradition exacts is a skepticism in action which listens for the unsaid in what has already been said. We are called to discover new and hidden possibilities in what we thought we knew and held dear. Tradition bequeaths to us its treasures, calling us to be cunning, resourceful, imaginative, and experimental in transforming it. This thrust within the tradition to transform itself has been named alternatively its "eschatological dimension" by religious adherents and "working toward justice" by legal scholars.

Why does tradition change? As we live more fully within traditions we gradually become aware of certain anomalies to it. Some beliefs and values seem to contradict others. This may occur because individuals are differently socialized, groups within the overall community have evolved in different ways, or the shadow distorts the authentic within the tradition. Once aware of the anomalies, we seek to resolve them. Secondly, tradition changes because we are thrown into the tradition at a particular juncture and thereby become aware that the wholeness towards which tradition aspires is not yet achieved. Injustices remain as surds to be overcome. We are never completely at one with what we are called to be; therefore, we can and must criticize. Finally, past and present human reflection and decisions are always finite. They define some considerations as relevant and others as irrelevant within limited horizons. Definition always leaves out some considerations which might very well have been significant in other circumstances. It is our task in the present to enable these long-buried items to come into the light of day.

How does a tradition change? Slowly, partially, and incrementally. Its movement is more like the gently flowing waters of a river in summertime than the raging floodwaters of spring. A tradition which transformed itself totally would no longer be that same tradition; it would have self-destructed. Traditions change by altering certain elements in the light of others deemed more basic. This is not to say that the pace of change is always the same or that the change might not be substantial over time. Revolutionary change does occur. But calls to revolution are grounded in the beliefs and values of the community, especially when the perception arises that those beliefs and values do not support given practices of authority. Revolutions likewise often prove not to have been so revolutionary as was originally claimed; tradition has a habit of reclaiming revolutions as its own. Whenever we find in an ancient text a meaning which strikes us as alien or read that our forebears esteem a human practice which appears reprehensible to us, we acknowledge that the tradition can and has changed substantially. Finally, the quest for justice and peace[13] proceeds in a piecemeal fashion.

---

[13] What in this text is being called *The Quest for Justice and Peace* has been elsewhere named *The Common Good*. Because the concept *Common Good* in too many minds stands for something fixed, static, and abstract, I have chosen the term that appears in this text for two principal reasons: *Quest* connotes a shared desire in the present for a better world; *Justice* and *Peace* denote the goals whose absence today elicits the desire. The use of "Quest for Justice and Peace" by no means involves a repudiation of the classical formulations of "Common Good." For Aristotle, individual happiness could only be achieved in a perfect society, a community of sufficient magnitude and complexity to foster the exercise of the virtuous life. In Augustine, individuals were fulfilled through a peace that reconciled conflicting claims. For Thomas Aquinas, the common good is an interchange of knowledge and good that transcends what the individual alone can achieve. This

Tradition strives not for utopias where life is perfect, but almost the same community where human practices are bettered.[14]

The Authoritative

The medium in which the tradition concretely appears is called the authoritative. The authoritative functions in relation to authority in a manner analogous to the part character plays in reference to freedom. The roles we play, the statuses we occupy, and the norms we follow in the playing and the occupying are embedded in the beliefs and values which are widely shared by members of a community. These values and beliefs constitute the final court of appeal in justifying practices of authority. They give birth to authority inasmuch as they promote cooperation and community over control and power. They are characterized by facticity; they are given— just *there* as the setting for judging the merits of existing or proposed rules inherent in such practices. Without the authoritative all our interests and desires, objectives and purposes would be of the moment.

These beliefs and values which constitute the authoritative are perceived by the members of any society to be "general facts of nature," the comparatively stable and widely accepted criteria which make possible reasoned and reasonable judgments concerning issues that arise about practices of authority. This usage of the notion of "nature" in relation to the authoritative needs further exploration. "General facts of nature" are neither what is given by nature nor something permanent and unchanging within the flux of history. What we call "natural" at any given time consists in what we have received as nature and what we have done with that gift. In community we draw upon both nature and culture, but in reality the two are indistinguishable. The "natural" in this sense is that without which human life cannot be conceived. These conceptions can and do change. One sad lesson of history is that the citizens of earlier civilizations could not imagine the good life without the presence of human slaves. Today we find the practice of slavery repugnant. Subsequent generations might find our acceptance of economically dependent people just as reprehensible. Also, people in the ancient world could not conceive of a drinking cup

---

good was realized in a community of friends which surpassed the sum of all the individual interests involved. On this subject, see William O'Neill's "No Amnesty for Sorrow." I am also indebted to Michael J. Buckley for his input on this matter.

[14] The principal influence on this section is Hans-Georg Gadamer, *Truth and Method.* I have also made use of Friedrich, Lash, Schaar, and Vining as well as Stephen Crites, "The Narrative Quality of Experience," *Journal of the American Academy of Religion* 39 (1971).

without inscriptions which linked quenching one's thirst with the play of the gods and the everyday activities of one's fellows. It is our sad loss that we prefer styrofoam cups. The "natural," then, is not some minimal (and usually highly abstract) set of norms which transcend history, but the whole constellation of beliefs and values that undergird the full panoply of our practices. The shared sense of the "natural" gives to any particular epoch its sense of being rather than of nothingness.

These beliefs and values are ideally animated by the real needs, desires, and aspirations of the people, supported by the physical, social, moral, and political resources of the community, and sustained by the requisite abilities, energies, discipline, and training of its members. In fact, they always look backwards toward our deepest affective needs, outward towards objects in the world, and forward to human fulfillments. They render possible the integration of the efforts of the members of a given community into fellowship. These beliefs and values are the place where challenges to authority are appropriately laid to rest. They serve us best when they serve our abiding interests, that is, when they define our ideals of individual and social existence so that the requirement of being human is satisfied.

Occasionally, the beliefs and values that constitute the authoritative (along with the roles, statuses, and norms in which they become enfleshed) are challenged. We live in a dynamic world of time and decay, of feedback and conflict. In critical periods we debate the merits of these beliefs and values, then alter or replace them. And the alterations or substitutions we make almost invariably require some changes in the practices of authority involved. The authoritative can change for two reasons. First of all, beliefs and values are always particular and, thus, never interchangeable with the good. Our beliefs and values, whether in isolation or as a sum total, never fully comprehend the thrust toward peace and justice. So, while the beliefs and values constitute the collective wisdom of ourselves and our predecessors, they are never absolutely conclusive. Secondly, in the case of *in* authority, while the authoritative connects with it, it is not the set of rules which establish and define that authority. No set of laws ever fully articulates the authoritative. In the case of *an* authority the same situation obtains because custom and convention are never fully convertible with fundamental beliefs and values. This gap between the authoritative and the rules internal to practices of authority allow the practices to differ from one community to another and from one period of history to another. And, as foundational beliefs and values evolve, so do our practices of authority.

The authoritative does not operate so much as a restraint on authority as give it room to breathe. When we attempt to tie it down once and for all, control it, and make all its elements fit neatly together, we construct not a mansion of authority where human freedom may roam, but a prison cell where liberty gasps for life. The authoritative achieves its purpose not primarily when its counsel is taken as to what should count and how each factor should be weighed but when human beings make free decisions. The freedom which issues in decisions has never been totally predictable nor enclosable in any conceptual system, no matter how sophisticated. Practices of authority and the authoritative which grounds them are likewise immune to such control.[15]

Legitimation

Since human tradition is a history not only of human goodness, but also of evil choices, and even of the preferment of evil to the good, practices of authority need to be carefully and continually distinguished from authoritarianism. Authoritarianism and ideology are the polar opposites of authority and its legitimation. Legitimacy is sometimes described as entitlement, what we earlier called the ability to speak in the name of. This description captures one pole of legitimation. Better definitions emphasize that legitimate exercises of authority issue a call to and awaken a sense of rightness. Signs that the requisite rightness obtains are that persuasion and not compulsion is used in the justification of authoritative acts, and that authority is exercised in the service of others. Any practice of authority contains its own limitations. It is impeded where coercion and inhibition are the rule, and prospers where it can be and is freely recognized.

Ordinarily, the legitimation of authority is a matter of trust. We take for granted that the roles, statuses, and norms which enflesh authority are correct. There is a presumption of the rightness of the rules inherent in the practices. The rules strike all participants as being what they ought to be. Of course the participants make these acts of faith in the conviction that the rules have been produced by reasonable people in the past and could be justified if necessary. They know that doubt and criticism make sense only in certain circumstances. Most human action presumes this faith or trust. It is present at the beginning of human community, making possible human discourse. We want to understand and to be persuaded. When we hear a statement or read a text, we assume that the voice speaking in what is said can be taken seriously, that the voice means what it says and is itself

---

[15] Again, Flathman is a dominant influence; besides Cameron, Friedrich, and Vining, I have also consulted E. M. Adams, "The Philosophical Grounds of the Present Crisis of Authority," *Authority,* ed. Harris, and W. H. Werkmeister, "The Function and Limits of Moral Authority," Ibid.

speaking in good faith. This presumption of truth (and, in the cases of practices of authority, of truth as rightness) undergirds all active life. It enables us to do hard work and press forward for self-betterment, to care about and take responsibility for what we do.

A practice of authority consists in how the ensemble of subscribers or participants constitute it by their words and deeds. There is no criterion independent of these words and deeds by which we can judge the legitimacy of a given practice.[16] Ordinarily, then, if the rules of the practice are followed, rightness is presumed and obedience becomes the appropriate behavior. Why is this so? Freedom, as we said earlier, is realization in life. It attains fulfillment in union. This is to say that when individuals band together in human community and make certain behaviors the way things are done (that is, develop practices), their wills are joined together in such a way that actions are executed with an economy of effort, thereby relieving us of the burden of having to work out each step along the way. Moreover, in community actions are performed in a recognizably human manner, that is, one agreed upon as appropriate among friends we trust. One unites one's own personal, individual freedom with others by allowing the habitualized patterns of behavior in the community to give shape to one's liberty. This shaping of freedom in community renders life feasible, and the concretization of our freedom in habitualized practices is called obedience.

While the confidence displayed in the execution of authority may be most pervasive and strong, the certainty involved in legitimacy is never absolute. Human practices are produced by human agents; hence, they are subject to some uncertainty, criticism, and, occasionally, change. We witness the aforementioned confidence in the resonance that obtains between leaders and followers where the communications that pass between the two parties make sense in such a way that both gain confidence in each other and in what is happening. The communications strike them as true and right. These sympathetic vibrations are possible because both parties share a common background and outlook. The transaction, however, is dynamic; meaning and influence flow back and forth between each part and transform both parties.

Another way of expressing the basis of trust in the rightness of rule is defining legitimacy as being capable of reasoned elaboration. Reason here means a socially valid body of knowledge, or what we have called the authoritative. "Reasoned elaboration" means that the practice of any specific

---

[16] In law, experts say the same thing when they insist that there is no independent inquiry into title.

authority could be justified by the giver or the receiver of the order by appeal to their common background or outlook. This background provides accounts of what counts as real, explanations of what is to be preferred, and visions of what is feasible in the future. When legitimacy is depicted as being capable of such reasoned elaboration, it is the "capable of" which deserves notice. People simply obey most orders in the confidence that they are right and could be justified. That external constraint, or sheer calculative interest, or deception, or manipulation is involved in the exercise of authority needs to be established. Otherwise we automatically assume that convincing reasons could be given for the rule of authority. But we also tacitly know that the obligation to conform with the requirements of rules and commands within the scope of the power of the one giving the command can never be exhaustively explained, analyzed, or justified in terms of the merits of such rules and commands alone. Explanations, analyses, and justifications have to cease somewhere. Legitimately, the burden of proof is on the one who objects to the rules.

This presumption of truth does not render practices of authority immune to questioning. Even in those cases where a ruler's communications are regularly credited with being capable of reasoned elaboration, we often observe that said ruler occasionally offers explicit reasons for his actions. We trust more fully those practices of authority where people do in fact demonstrate the rationality of what is transpiring. So, far from being mutually incompatible, the presumption of rightness and the giving of reasons often go hand in hand.

In practices of authority, unquestioning trust and giving reasons exist in a relationship of complementarity. If either pole of the relationship is suppressed, practices of authority become destabilized. The character of reasoned elaboration varies as the community is born, grows, is transformed, disintegrates, and is reconstituted. In stable times, being reasonable about authority for superior and subject alike is largely a habit; legitimacy is generally perceived to be coterminous with custom (in the case of *an* authority) or legality (where *in* authority obtains). In revolutionary situations, on the other hand, not only the rules for the exercise of authority but also the very practices of authority themselves can be challenged, changed and/or replaced. In such periods we require theories to justify our obedience and to render the power involved legitimate. In such circumstances, legitimacy is achieved only when the rules inherent in the practices of authority are placed in principle beyond the individual (that is, self-centered) wills of all the participants in the practices.

The obedience that undergirds most authority is never wholly blind. When the potential for criticizing the merits of the rules and of the practices

asserted or presumed by authorities disappears, so does authentic authority and empowerment and obligation. Manipulation and coercion and abject submission soon replace them. While widespread and continuing
approval of the substance of commands is a condition for the continuity of
the practices, it is not a sufficient reason. Only the great overarching purposes (the good in the form of the striving for peace and justice) and the
union of individual members in friendship (realization in life) provide a
sufficient basis for continuity of practices. Whenever we have mechanical
repetition or simply blind obedience we can reasonably suspect that justice, peace, and/or freedom have been sacrificed.

Doubts and questions, however, do arise. People do become aware that
certain practices of authority or the rules according to which the practices
are conducted are no longer congruent with the fundamental beliefs and values of the community. Then reason, grounded in the authoritative, examines
the background of the outlooks we share, explains or explores preferences
for various alternatives, and looks into the implications and consequences of
the alternatives. Reason aims to lead the community from drunkenness to
sobriety. Eventually one or some other alternative is selected, having gained
the support of the majority of the participants in the practice. They reach this
point when the new or modified practice strikes them as "natural."

When do doubts and questions make sense? Given the almost infinite
cunning of human reason, any response to this question needs to be carefully framed. We might suggest, however, that doubts and questions come
reasonably to the fore when either the quest for peace and justice is frus-
trated or the liberty of individuals is suppressed in a practice of authority. In
the first case some participants in the practice are treated unequally, undue
or uncalled for force is used, or the scope of *in* authority has been unneces-
sarily broadened. If individual liberty is suppressed, initiative is not permitted in the exercise of authority, some are unreasonably excluded from
participation, or individual autonomy has not been respected. Often the
source of our displeasure with authority is that both the quest for justice
and peace and the inviolability of freedom have been violated in its exercise, for these overarching purposes of our lives complement each other.

Doubts and questions about authority are always particular. Methodical
doubt is not a reasonable behavior. In taking this position we are objecting to
methodical doubt as an intellectual ideal; habits of doubt may be justified in
certain circumstances, for example, when the giver of commands displays
the characteristics of a tyrant or the receivers have shown a consistent pattern of being lackeys or the very patterns of authority in a particular society
have clearly become bankrupt. But we need to notice that rather than me-
thodically doubting *all* authority people normally evaluate and criticize one

practice of authority on the basis of its similarities to and differences from another practice deemed an exemplar. For instance, people who live in democratic societies often criticize exercises of religious authority as authoritarian even in those churches which have a long tradition of paternalism. In short, reasoning about authority, and especially being critical about it, is very concrete and particular rather than abstract and universal.

When the proper interplay between trust and criticism occurs in community, legitimacy promotes vigor in life. This is so because authority makes it possible for individuals living together to achieve what they could never do in isolation. This union of hearts and minds issues in a public enthusiasm which commands the allegiance of both the led and their leaders. Their lives in community take on the character of enchantment. Such enchantment, whether actual and felt, or remembered or hoped for, draws out of us actions in which we live more fully and without reservation. Vigor in life is not accessible to individuals as such, but only to those joined together as communities in practices of authority. The ideal of authority does not foster communities where cold respect based on fear and expressed in wariness is rampant, but communities where the call for peace and justice and the enhancement of freedom brings the members more fully alive.[17]

Dissent

Tradition is an evolving reality. The authoritative is both the standard by which practices of authority are to be evaluated and is itself capable of being called into question (at least in its particulars). The beliefs and values which compose the authoritative are both plausible and feasible, but they are not final. The conversation among ourselves about our inheritance and our destiny goes on and on and on. The quest for peace and justice is never fully achieved; nor does freedom in community ever attain its fullness in friendship in the world we presently inhabit.

Practices of authority are complex, multifaceted phenomena. Judgments about their rightness are governed by criteria which are difficult to apply. Grounded, reasoned judgments of agreement and disagreement seem to be a permanent feature of our lives together. Further, the good

---

[17] Besides Flathman, Friedrich, Herbst, Schaar, and Vining, Bernard Lonergan, "Dialectic of Authority," *Authority,* ed. Adelman; and Walter Molinski, "Authority," *Encyclopedia of Theology (A Concise Sacramentum Mundi),* ed. Karl Rahner (N.Y.: Seabury, 1975); and Thomas O'Dea, "Authority and Freedom in the Church: Tension, Balance, Contradiction, an Historical-Sociological View," *Who Decides for the Church?,* ed. James Coriden (Hartford, Conn.: Canon Law Society of America, 1971).

person is never exactly the same as the good citizen, soldier, bureaucrat, etc.—or even the good citizen in the good society. The best among us always transcend the standards of the community even while they benefit from it and perform their duties within it. And we are better off because this is so.

Initially, authority requires dissent for two reasons. First, the quest for peace and justice, while a permanent feature of human existence, is never finally concretized, especially in the light of the complexity that is authority. Too many agencies compete for the upper hand in those larger societies which alone might bring about this utopian dream. Secondly, freedom is never subsumed under authority, but remains in dialectical relationship with it. Given the resources at the beck and call of authority, the danger persists that authority will attempt to quiet, not promote, individual liberty.

Estrangement from the human ideals of a community of peace and justice and of the fully free individual will be with us always. Mystery and guilt, comedy and tragedy compete upon the stage of human affairs. Our human fate is a state of qualified unhappiness in which we try every day to win good from evil and affirm beauty in spite of ugliness. Our deepest secret is that the sacred and the obscene coexist in the human psyche.

There are two other reasons why dissent must accompany authority on its pilgrimage through history. The process of socializing individuals into society attempts to ward off the threat of chaos in human interactions by raising certain roles, statuses, and norms above ourselves as individual actors. They are given a life of their own, an objectivity. When these roles, statuses, and norms become isolated from the energies that beget change and take on the character of independence from all actors (what sociologists call alienation—a state in which we forget that we ourselves have constructed these realities), two things occur. First, cultural achievement is separated from natural gift and the practices of authority become disembodied realities. In this circumstance we prefer our own achievement to what is graciousness. The Protestant reformers counseled us well to beware of works-righteousness, the theological equivalent of such alienation. Secondly, the roles, statuses, and norms cease to be finite realities and take on a definitive character. The way things are becomes the way things ought to be, and morality reduces itself to plausibility. This quest for atemporality is actually a forgetfulness of our finitude, who we are. We forget that human existence, especially in its communal dimension, is being unto death. To enshrine a particular practice of authority as *the* practice (in the sense that it transcends change) constitutes an attempt to ward off the threat of death. Grace and death are as much a part of the human condition as culture and structure. Dissent renders practices of authority responsive to the forces of chaos at both ends of the temporal spectrum. Thus, a good question to gauge whether authority is functioning well is not so much "What end or purpose does it serve?" as "Of what conflicts is it the scene?"

Without dissent obligation dissolves into mere convention, and rules of authority into laws which guide us down a path to a place where the living dead dwell. On a pragmatic level, readiness to consider disobedience and put those considerations into action does seem to relieve severe conflicts between authority and individual agency and keep authority figures themselves within limits. Without any kind of dissent, a community soon faces a Hobson's choice between tyranny and anarchy. Criticism and, if necessary, disobedience constitute appropriate responses to a practice of authority which yields unacceptable (because self-interested) commands. Dissent in word and deed, in such cases, attempts to restore authenticity to authority. Obedience can only be, in the final analysis, to what I can and ought to give agreement. Obedience is sterile unless it unites us to our fellows in conversation. And the law of conversation is not that it is an exchange among the like-minded, but that it enables us to know our own identities in simultaneity with what is other. Thus, rhetoric is the field on which the game of authority is played.[18]

[18] Flathman, Friedrich, Schaar, Vining.

CHAPTER 4

The First Millennium

Introduction

In chapter two we asserted that Church authority is sacramental. By this assertion we meant not only that the paradigms for thinking about ecclesiastical authority are the celebration of the Eucharist and the preaching of the Word, but also the concept *sacrament* best illumines how authority in general (chapter three) becomes authority in the Church. In sacraments, we encounter in the Spirit the risen Christ as the graciousness of God while we speak human words and do certain gestures. These words and gestures immerse us in the human condition, more specifically, in the temporal dimension of our lives. Thus, we also maintained in chapter two that the nature of Church authority could not be derived philosophically or theologically, but required a careful tracing of the development of ecclesiastical authority over the last twenty centuries. It is to the study of that development that we now turn.

Authority in the New Testament

In the New Testament, authority as such is not a primary datum. The word for *authority, exousia,* is used ninety-five times in all the books, but only a handful of those usages (less than ten) are relevant for our consideration.[1] Moreover, in the Gospels, *exousia* often bears negative connotations as the kind of "lording it over others" that Gentile leaders are known for—a behavior altogether unworthy of Jesus' disciples. Authority in the New Testament perspective is sustained by the eschatological orientation of the Church. When tensions arise between the eschatological goal

---

[1] The classic treatment of the history of authority in the Church remains Yves Congar's magisterial essay, "The Historical Development of Authority in the Church: Points for Reflection," *Problems of Authority,* ed. John M. Todd (London: Helicon Press, 1962) 119–50.

and the actual performance of the Church, persons in authority function to recall all members to the true goal of their lives together. Such is their primary function.

The forms in which authority is exercised in the New Testament are extremely complex. Paul mentions nine ways in which authority functions among the Corinthians, three of which (being an apostle, a prophet, a teacher) seem to take precedence over the others which are nonetheless still authenticated in the Spirit. Some communities, especially those in which the members expected the imminent return of Jesus, appear to have known practically no structure at all. Churches which became conscious that the interval between the resurrection and the parousia would be of some duration did evolve structures which were primitive by comparison with those we know today. Probably the most structured church in the New Testament was the community which gave us the Pastoral epistles. Its structures reveal how intimate the connection between authority and preaching and teaching was for that church.[2]

Wherever authority appears in the New Testament, the overriding conviction is that it derives from God the Father as its ultimate source and functions at the service of all members of the Church. The assumed pattern is that people in authority have been sent by Jesus, God's beloved son, and exercise their oversight as gifted by the Spirit.

The context for any understanding of New Testament authority is the sovereignty of God: God created the world, continues to rule over its history, and more recently has revealed the fullness of the divine salvific power in the coming of Jesus Christ. The kingly rule of God calls for a radical transformation of heart in men and women, a conversion which now amounts to following Jesus Christ. Jesus possesses authority not on his own, but as the Son of the Father. He displays this authority in the perfect concordance between the message he proclaims (the rule of God is at hand) and his behavior, especially the events of his death and resurrection where the rule of God is perfectly realized. During his public ministry he exercised authority by curing sickness, exorcising demons, welcoming the unclean into God's love, and forgiving sins. All these activities in this period were confined largely to the people of Israel. After his exaltation, Jesus' authority becomes universal and he bestows the Holy Spirit as his greatest gift upon the disciples he loved. The Spirit takes hold of the entire community (or, in Matthew, the Twelve who represent the new People of God) and its action is varied and wide-ranging. It inspires the Scriptures, guides community

---

[2] Myles Bourke, "Reflections on Church Order in the New Testament," *Catholic Biblical Quarterly* 30 (1968) 493–511.

leaders, and dwells in each believer. It is the *same* spirit who inspires, guides, and dwells. Though the Scriptures, leaders, and ordinary believers have different functions in the community, each is somehow endowed in the Spirit with the authority which the exalted Christ alone can grant because of his perfect union with the Father. This majestic vision of the Godhead and its salvific work among men and women forms the background of all understanding of authority in the books of the New Testament: it is first and foremost stewardship.[3]

A correlative for authority in the New Testament is authenticity as exemplified in Jesus as the beloved Son of God and his followers as disciples of Jesus. Jesus himself acted with assurance and decisiveness. He settled the divorce question (Mark 10:2-9) in a manner unthinkable for a scribe and expelled demons in a way that demonstrated that he clearly had authority over them (Mark 1:23-28 or 5:1-20). But it was the fact that he lived the rule of God the way it should be lived that best exemplified his authority. There was no disparity between what he said and what he did. In both his words and deeds, he was totally consumed with the rule of God, so much so that the message and the works drew attention to the rule of God, and not to him. And even they pointed beyond themselves to the source of Jesus' authority—his Father. He most fully displayed the nature of his authority in the paschal mystery. There a central maxim of his ministry—"Whoever would gain his life must lose it, and whoever loses his life for my sake will gain life eternal"—was fulfilled in his person. He laid down his life in obedience to the Father and for the redemption of all. On the cross he revealed that his was a total union with the Father and he challenged all his followers to go and do likewise. Neither his ministry nor his dying were a haphazard acting out of a role that might have been otherwise, but a demonstration of the way to live truly in the presence of God. In his life, death, and resurrection, he reveals both the love of God for us and the appropriate response to that love. The claim he lays upon followers, however, is a claim made in love. It is given without guile or coercion and calls for a free, though total, response. In his resurrection, Jesus is empowered in God to make everyone a son or daughter of God.

In the Church all members share in the authority given by the risen Christ (John 20:9-23; Acts 2:1-4). Authority is his collective endowment. Each one receives a share in it at baptism and in the continued workings of the Spirit in each for the sake of the whole community. All are called to build up the body of Christ. The Church lives in the presence of its risen

---

[3] David Stanley, "Authority in the Church: A New Testament Reality," *Catholic Biblical Quarterly* 29 (1967) 555–73.

Lord, ever conscious that his lordship is not perfectly realized, but convinced that its efforts here and now as graced in the Spirit contribute to that realization. The Church urges its members to loyal adherence, commitment to an unknown future, and the giving of themselves. This faith, hope, and love is achieved through union with God and sharing in the mind of Christ, placing our confidence in God alone and being possessed by God's truth. It is finally revealed in the works of justice and mercy.

But these gifts of faith, hope, and love are not given to Christians only for their own betterment. The Church is a community of sinners called to be disciples of Jesus who receive the Good News in order to communicate it to others. The Church commends its message to others by word and example. Endowed by the Holy Spirit, it looks and hopes for a response in the same Spirit from those who hear its witness. After the example of its Lord, the Church speaks its truth to free human persons.[4]

The nature of this service to which Church authority is called takes as its paradigm the Parable of the Good Samaritan (Luke 10:29-37). There, as Søren Kierkegaard observed, the Samaritan does not turn to the man fallen among thieves as an *alter ego,* but lets this half-dead wretch appear in his uniqueness so that the Samaritan allows this other person to expand what it means to be a Samaritan. Just as the Word of God became truly other in the incarnation, so the followers of Jesus are summoned to become their neighbor who expands the disciple's identity as an *alter Christus.* In the incarnation Jesus embodied what God clearly is not—a creature—even to the extent that he identified himself with those whose very creatureliness appeared most opposed to the divine purposes in creation. Jesus' association with the ill, the possessed, and the outcasts was, therefore, essential to his very being—becoming what God is not, because Jesus entered into the entirety of the human condition, including all its negativities, even death. In his death he became permanently identified with the suffering in the world, and, by rising from the dead, bestowed his Spirit upon them so they are other Christs by being neighbors in need to all who have compassion on them. The service, then, that characterizes Church authority has a particular bent: the neighbor in need mediates to members of the Church the graciousness of God in Christ.[5]

---

[4] John Ashton, "Authority in the Gospels," *The Way* 12 (1972) 211–21, and Robert Murray "Authority and the Spirit in the New Testament," *Authority in a Changing Church,* John Dalrymple and others (London: Sheed and Ward, 1968) 12–38.

[5] William O'Neill, "No Amnesty For Sorrow" (to be published in *Theological Studies*); and John Donahue, "Who Is My Enemy? The Parable of the Good Samaritan and the Love of Enemies," *The Love of Enemy and Nonretaliation in*

As an example of the authority of discipleship the New Testament commends to us the Apostle Paul. The claim Paul consistently makes for his authority is based not primarily on his own apostleship but on his unswerving fidelity to Christ as illustrated in his suffering with Christ on behalf of his converts. His life constitutes living testimony before all that Christ is alive in him. He has totally surrendered himself to Christ Jesus, and only on this basis does Paul challenge his fellow Christians to a fuller participation in the Christ-life and correct their mistaken interpretations of what is asked of them. Throughout his letters breathes the conviction that Paul is completely dependent on the risen Lord. Union with God is the source of his strength and the bulwark of his mission. Though Paul does on occasion appeal to his apostleship for authority, his letters betray a pronounced preference on his part for standing on the spiritual gifts he has received, the blessings bestowed on his labors including his sacrificial witness, the love and devotion he has shown in these labors, and even his obvious weaknesses. He refrains from claiming rights and praises giving as an alternative to receiving. Paul can be quite peremptory in his demands for obedience. Yet he is careful not to separate himself from or place himself above the community. He recognizes that all members also possess gifts from the Spirit. He patiently explains his reasons for a certain course of action in the confidence that his hearers, too, can discern where the Spirit is leading. If pushed to the limit Paul is very exacting of obedience. In those passages where he so acts, his arguments are founded on his understanding of the gospel as well as on his apostleship. Finally, Paul exercises authority always in the light of the total Christ. The building up of the body of Christ is his sole and perpetual concern.[6]

Being authoritative in the New Testament is a consequence of having faith, with the result that others can be confident that Christians are empowered in the Spirit of God. This empowerment is displayed in the ability of all the first Christians to proclaim the word of the Lord boldly and openly even in the face of a hostile or indifferent audience. It is modeled on the sovereign freedom of Jesus who made bold to speak the truth candidly to people who were opposed to his message, even in the prospect of imminent death. This empowerment is nourished on the experience of each believer who, in prayer, gains access to God as a loving Father rather than a distant

---

the New Testament, ed. Willard Swartley (Louisville: Westminster/John Knox, 1992), plus *The Gospel In Parable* (Philadelphia: Fortress, 1988) 128–34.

[6] Ernest Best, "Paul's Apostolic Authority," *Journal for the Study of the New Testament* 27 (1986) 3–25, and Sean Freyne, "The Exercise of Christian Authority According to the New Testament," *Irish Theological Quarterly* 37 (1970) 93–117.

monarch to be approached only in fear. Jesus' word is most perfectly proclaimed in the context of the Lord's Supper. In the final analysis, the paradigmatic expressions of the authorization the Church has received are the proclamation of the Word and the celebration of the Eucharist.[7]

The New Testament itself is a perfect example of bold proclamation and is likewise a preeminent instance of how the primitive Church understood its authority. The overriding conviction that undergirds all the writings is that the earthly Jesus lived for the Church to come, that the risen Lord and his present will for the Church constitute the call to testimony. While the various authors reverence the words of Jesus and the apostolic preachers, they apply these words to the present situation of the local community with much ingenuity. They aim at a Spirit-filled interpretation of the meaning here and now for the words of Jesus, Peter, and the other apostles, and not for factual exactitude in reporting. In the composition of the New Testament, authority is thoroughly opposed to rote repetition and nostalgia.[8]

The New Testament does propose a style for the exercise of Christian authority: service. Service is opposed to any "lording it over" other people, a familiar practice in the ancient world. Service is furthermore a paradoxical style for the Church to have adopted in the first century. Service was not held in high esteem by prospective pagan converts of the first century because it did not befit a free person. The Jews at the time recognized a value in service, but generally restricted its benefits to pious Jews. Nonetheless, the primitive Church summoned its members to a universal service. It did so in the conviction that Jesus' kingship was revealed in self-sacrificing love. This love placed him at the service of both God his Father and the disciples around him. It could be no different for anyone who would later be his disciple. Superiority in the church demanded humility. Luke, who knew a local church with incipient structures, emphasizes that leaders should never understand themselves apart from the community and are called to greater than usual vigilance and responsibility for the community (cf. the parable of the unjust steward). For all New Testament writers, the Cross constitutes the controlling image for this summons to service. There Jesus laid down his life in obedience to his Father and for the sake of those he loved and even in this extreme situation issued a summons that could be responded to in freedom.[9]

Some primitive churches did know more structure. As early as Paul, we find local churches which recognized the apostle himself as their father

---

[7] Stanley Marrow, *Speaking the Word Fearlessly* (N.Y.: Paulist, 1982).

[8] Ashton, Freyne, Murray, and Stanley.

[9] Ashton, Freyne, Murray, and Stanley.

in the faith or superior and knew administrating as one of the charisms. The Pastoral epistles provide us with what is probably our fullest picture of structure in some of the early churches. There the problem of succession in right doctrine looms large. How will the Church maintain itself in the gospel and the apostolic preaching and safeguard itself from corruption by false teachers? The solution lies in selecting men of upright life and designating them as presbyter-overseers by the laying on of hands. Their leadership, but foremost their preaching and teaching, create a medium for continuity in the faith.

From the very beginning authority in the Church was linked with preaching and teaching (the two are not clearly distinguishable). The Church predicated this link on the fact that Jesus preached and taught. On this basis, it developed as an ideal that the message and the messenger were to be as close to identical to each other as possible. John emphasizes that teaching is a Spirit-guided process into the truth which belongs to the community as a whole. Matthew, especially at the end of his gospel, links the proclamation of the gospel, baptism of the nations, and teaching what Jesus taught into a composite whole. He further ties the authority of Jesus' disciples intimately with that of the risen Christ himself. For Matthew, authority in the Church is both universal and for the ages. He, of course, knew what Paul had earlier exemplified: that teaching as Jesus did always requires of the teacher that he or she draw new from the old.

Did people ever resist this teaching? We have good reason to think so from the preoccupation with false teaching throughout the New Testament and, especially, from two passages which deal with excommunication or expulsion from the eucharistic community. In 1 Corinthians 5, Paul, in a most solemn fashion, excommunicates the incestuous man. Yet he also asks that the community concur in his verdict and pronounce the sentence in assembly. Thereby he does not separate himself from the Corinthians but acknowledges that they all share in the same baptism and in the same Spirit and confess the one Lord in an identical faith.[10]

In Matthew 18 rules are laid down for expulsion from the community. The context for such action is the pervasively forgiving attitude of the Lord. Expulsion can never be lightly administered; it is always the last resort. The power to take punitive action, however, is from the Lord who concurs in its rightful exercise. The principle involved in such action is the Eucharist

[10] Myles Bourke, "Collegial Decision-Making in the New Testament," *Who Decides for the Church,* ed. James Coriden (Hartford, Conn.: Canon Law Society of America, 1971) 1–13, and George MacRae, "Shared Responsibility—Some New Testament Perspectives," *Shared Responsibility in the Local Church,* eds. Charles Curran and George Dywer (Chicago: Chicago Studies, 1970) 3–15.

where the command to love which binds the assembly together precludes the presence of one who egregiously offends against that love.

Finally, no Roman Catholic consideration of New Testament authority can ignore Matthew 16. The text in question should, in my opinion, be read from verses 13 through 23. Such a reading brings out that Peter is not only the rock but also the stumbling block, not only the one to whom the Father in heaven has given special revelation but also one who is on the side of human beings, not only the only person in the Gospels to receive a dominical blessing as an individual but also the Satan who tempts Jesus to abandon his mission. Peter is both a singular sinner and a particularly graced saint. For his faith, Peter does receive real authority to bind and loose and to carry the keys of the kingdom, and he is granted these powers in the perpetual struggle against evil. We also need to remember that Matthew 16 was applied variously in the early Church: to every believer (in the East), to every bishop (in Africa), and to the Bishop of Rome (in the West). This memory should warn us that any succession in Peter's primacy must always be understood in terms of collegiality with all bishops and that union which all the baptized share in Christ Jesus. In the Matthean passage as elsewhere in the New Testament, where, in all the major passages, a rebuke by Jesus accompanies the assignment of a special role to Peter, Petrine primacy is not presented as first and foremost a juridical point. A better scriptural argument for and understanding of Peter's primacy could be grounded in the fact that the story of Peter is always included in the telling of what God has done in Jesus of Nazareth.[11]

[11] Besides the works already cited, the following also proved helpful in compiling this New Testament Section: David Bossman, "Authority and Tradition in First Century Judaism and Christianity," *Biblical Theology Bulletin* 17 (1987) 3–9; Joseph Fitzmyer, "The Office of Teaching in the Christian Church According to the New Testament," *Teaching Authority and Infallibility in the Church,* eds. Paul Empie, Austin Murphy, and Joseph Burgess (Minneapolis: Augsburg, 1978) 186–212 (and John Reumann, "Teaching Office in the New Testament? A Response to Professor Fitzmyer's Essay," Ibid., 213–31); Bengt Holmberg, *Paul and Power* (Philadelphia: Fortress, 1980); John McKenzie, *Authority in the Church* (N.Y.: Sheed and Ward, 1966); Wayne Meeks, *The First Urban Christians* (New Haven, Conn.: Yale University Press, 1983) 111–39; James Reese, "How Matthew Portrays the Communication of Christ's Authority," *Biblical Theology Bulletin* 7 (1977) 139–44; Elisabeth Schussler-Fiorenza, *In Memory of Her* (N.Y.: Crossroad, 1983) 285–342; John Schultz, *Paul and the Anatomy of Apostolic Authority* (Cambridge: Cambridge University Press, 1975); and Eduard Schweizer, *Church Order in the New Testament,* trans. Frank Clark (Naperville: A. R. Allensen, 1961); Hans von Campenhausen, *Ecclesiastical Authority and Spiritual Power in the Church of the First Three Centuries* (Stanford: Stanford University Press, 1969);

The Postapostolic Era: The Ascendancy of Monoepiscopacy

In the second century the structure of authority in the Christian Church underwent a profound alteration. At the beginning of the century two forms of government existed side by side in the church: leadership by a group of elders acting corporately and leadership by a single bishop. By the end of the same century, the latter form, monarchical episcopacy (i.e., governance of the local church by a single leader), seems to have taken hold everywhere. The first form, government by a college of elders or presbyters, appears to have been taken over by the early Christians from their Jewish forebears. It seemed natural to select senior outstanding and honored figures in the community to exercise authority collectively. *1 Clement* tells us that it was the task of the presbyters to "present the gifts"; that is, they were leaders of worship. Elsewhere we learn that leaders of the church were especially charged with the supervision of doctrine. Ignatius of Antioch (roughly the year 110) testifies to the early presence of monarchical episcopacy. He knows a number of local churches where bishops, presbyters, and deacons exist as distinct ministries, with the bishop the undisputed leader of the church who makes decisions and gives commands. His primary task is to preserve the unity of his church which is the harmony and fundamental agreement of an abundance of parts. In one letter Ignatius compares church harmony to the harmony that several musical instruments achieve with one another.

By the early third century Hippolytus can take for granted that monoepiscopacy exists everywhere in the Church. He tells us that the local bishop was a high priest, a teacher, and a watchman; that is, he presided at the Eucharist, taught the Scriptures as interpreted according to the traditions of the community (certainly in sermons, but probably also outside the liturgy), and baptized, plus dismissed and reconciled sinners. For Hippolytus, the bishop is primarily a liturgical leader who feeds his flock on doctrine and guards this doctrine from infection and error. Hippolytus also mentions that the bishop is a mediator representing God to the church and the church to God, especially in the Eucharist where the bishop presents the church's self-offering to God and receives from God in the name of the community that gift now identified with Christ's own self-offering. Many experts have conjectured that there probably was a transitional stage between monoepiscopacy and corporate presbyterial government in those churches where the latter form had at first obtained. It perhaps became customary for a single elder to act *ex officio* as the head of the whole body along the lines of the High Priest in the Sanhedrin at Jerusalem.

John Baldovin, *City, Church, and Renewal* (Washington, D.C.: Pastoral Press, 1991) 151–70.

The reasons for the alteration in government were multiple. The *Didache* tells us that government in the church is necessary if the local community is to remain stable in the face of itinerant apostles, prophets, and teachers. As the second century progressed the problem became heretics, in particular the Gnostics. The bishop became the symbol of unity and the public guarantee of faith against the anarchy created by heresy. In the very early Church apostolicity was an overriding concern. *1 Clement* tells us that as the Father sent Christ, so Christ sent the apostles who selected leaders for the communities they founded. Irenaeus speaks of a rule of faith, the normative and public teaching of the apostolic churches (probably in a primitive creedal form), and offers a list of bishops at Rome, tracing the present incumbent back to the apostles Peter and Paul. Tertullian informs us that the apostles knew all from Jesus and transmitted that knowledge intact and undiluted to the churches they founded which continue to teach this message publicly to all who will listen. This apostolicity constituted continuity in the local church's teaching of the Scriptures. This continuity in tradition could be traced back to the founding apostles and through them to God and his Christ. Against the Gnostics who had argued that they were heirs to a secret tradition passed on to them through a succession of witnesses extending back to the apostles themselves, the local churches stressed that this tradition was not an esoteric teaching but the public handing on of what had been received. This public character was embodied in the community's leader, the bishop as successor in a long line of such leaders, all of whom had passed on faithfully what they had received. Thus, this succession was a continuity in faith, that is, a faithful handing on, and not a merely juridical reality. The bishop symbolized to all who had ears to hear that the local church had faithfully preserved the teachings of the apostles in their integrity and unity. As a consequence, bishops were expected to be instructed, informed and spiritual.

There can be no question that the growth of the Church during this century facilitated the growth of monoepiscopacy. The original community was forced to spawn satellite parishes, and the designation of one figure in the community to supervise the more complex reality of the Church that resulted seemed to make sense. But there was another reason for the change which appears even more crucial: the early Church was also preoccupied with the issue of unity. Sometimes, monoepiscopacy was justified because the oneness of God demanded it. The early Church was concerned that its great Jewish heritage, monotheism, along with the unity of the local church in the midst of the forces of chaos around it, should be symbolized in a public and unambiguous manner. The symbol the churches collectively chose was the monarchical bishop. The bishop was a unique organ of the Holy Spirit indwelling the whole Church; one bishop represented the unity of the members with one another and with God.

Finally, it should be noted that the lifelong tenure accorded to the local bishop was unique in ancient social order. Neither the Jewish high priest nor imperial officials had lifelong terms. The emergence of monoepiscopacy cannot be explained on the basis of imitation of extraecclesial models.[12]

The early Church was by and large composed of local assemblies— concrete, individual congregations gathered around their bishops through whom the members were physically and spiritually united to one another and to Christ. Even when the original congregation spawned daughter assemblies, members saw the church primarily as a local reality including the individual assemblies. At this time it was generally assumed that uniformity of lifestyle throughout the universal Church was neither necessary nor viable. In the second century, each local church might have its own canon of Scriptures, its own unique baptismal creed, its own liturgy plus its own peculiar discipline. At the apex of the whole community, as its leader of worship and in teaching, stood the bishop. As president of the worshiping assembly, he was at one with all the members and thus able to speak in the name of all. In the liturgy itself his "I" was indistinguishable from the community's "We" as exemplified in the common liturgical practice of the bishop's saying at the beginning of the Eucharistic Prayer, "Let us make Eucharist," and the assembly's response, "It is meet and right." This is not to say that there existed no local variations in the image of the bishop. At Rome he was first and foremost a leader of a cult; in Syria a spiritual example and sacral focus; and in Asia Minor the ordained preacher of the apostolic teaching.

Whatever the local image of the bishop, his personal qualities had to meet high standards. Bishops were to be spiritual men, assiduous in their study of Scripture, fasting, and hospitality. Other qualities frequently mentioned are that the bishop be a good listener and willing helper, able to edify all the members. He was not to be interested in his own gain but

---

[12] Henry Chadwick, "The Role of the Christian Bishop in Ancient Society," 35th Colloquium (Berkeley: Center for Hermeneutical Studies, 1980) 1–14; Gregory Dix, *Jurisdiction in the Early Church* (London: Faith House, 1975); Robert Eno, "Shared Responsibility in the Early Church," *Shared Responsibility in the Local Church,* 17–30; John Lynch, "Co-Responsibility in the First Five Centuries: Presbyteral Colleges and the Election of Bishops," *Who Decides for the Church?,* 14–52; and von Campenhausen. In the historical sections of this and the next chapter, I am making use of multiple sources. It seemed best to acknowledge the sources in groups rather than footnoting each specific usage.

concerned for the welfare of all, being thirsty after justice. That many fulfilled these prerequisites is illustrated in the advice given two centuries later by Propus to Ambrose upon the latter's appointment as prefect in Milan: "Act not as a judge but like a bishop."[13]

The bishop, furthermore, linked the local assembly to the universal Church because he belonged to the fraternity of bishops. This unity was a communion in faith, and it needs to be noted that, from the beginning, the entire Church was less tolerant of local differences in doctrine than of other variations. Already in the second century, the bishops of particular regions gathered in synods to affirm a uniform faith, especially against the Montanists, and even in some cases of discipline if these were sufficiently connected with a central tenet of the faith, as the synods to discuss the date of Easter toward the end of the second century illustrate.

Yet the bishop remained, above all, the president of the local eucharistic assembly, alone empowered by God at the church's prayer to perform the various liturgies for the whole assembly which was the body of Christ. On this basis he became leader, guide, and teacher of all the members both as individuals and in union with one another. In fact, one of the principal ways in which these early local churches attained communion with each other was through the exchange of their various liturgical riches.[14]

The principal power which the bishop possessed was the power of the keys. He controlled membership in the church by determining who had the right to join in the worship, to enjoy the overall church fellowship, and to share in the intercessions and sanctity of the assembly. When this power of the keys was combined with the power of binding and loosing, the right to forgive sins in God's name came to the fore. The gift of the Spirit in the episcopal consecration communicated above all the power over sin exercised in admittance to baptism and excommunication from the eucharistic assembly. For most Christians, the episcopal power of the keys was a matter of life and death. They literally believed that the bishop had the sacred power to grant or refuse entry not only into the community but into heaven as well and they often heeded the bishop out of fear of divine retribution.

The power of the keys in the early Church was not any unconstrained power of the kind usually associated with tyrants. The ordination prayers of Hippolytus indicate that what we call the day-to-day government of the

---

[13] Congar, "The Historical Development of Authority in the Church: Points for Reflection," 125, 130–31. Scholars of this period emphasize that the evidence for the style of early Church life is meager. The presentations here follow what scholars generously depict, but one suspects that Church life in that period was more fluid.

[14] Chadwick and Dix.

church was corporately exercised by the presbyterate around the bishop. Thus, the episcopal practice of power of the keys occurred when the bishop proclaimed what had been jointly decided by the whole presbyterate. This emphasis on proclamation brings out the mystical character of the power of the keys. It was not a matter of the bishop's having jurisdiction over the individual members, but of his being able to speak an efficacious word. Thus, there existed a powerful motivation for the bishop to live up to the traditional ideals of the community. If there appeared an obvious gap between his deeds and his word, there existed a good reason for Christians to doubt whether a particular episcopal decree was rendered in the Spirit of God.[15]

In the second century, Hegesippus, a Jewish Christian and extensive traveler, found widespread uniformity in the teaching of local churches in contrast to the contradictions rampant in what the Gnostics taught. He observed that the local bishops by word and example drew their listeners into a union of faith. He attributed this union to the communion they had with Christ. In his remarks Hegesippus highlights the importance of the bishop as teacher, his concern to be of one mind with both the surrounding local churches but also with the mind of Christ as it was transmitted to and through the apostles. As the century progressed the Church grew in the conviction that its tradition had been laid down once and for all, was known to all the churches in a recognizably identical form, and was the most prized possession it could bequeath to the next generation.

At the outset of the third century Tertullian testifies to the belief that all Christians participate in the priesthood of Christ by virtue of their baptism. A more important witness from Africa is Cyprian. According to Cyprian, the unity of a local congregation comes from its communal subjection to a single bishop. In submitting itself to that bishop, the congregation submits itself to God. The bishop himself is responsible to God and belongs to a college of bishops whose covenant binding themselves together in mutual association constitutes the universal unity of the Church. Cyprian interprets the Petrine commission in Matthew 16:18-19 to mean that Christ bestowed power on Peter not as the superior of the other apostles, but to symbolize unity as the basic value in the Church.

The Church, for Cyprian, is a corporate body with a structure and constitution which were established by Christ and obtained among the churches of apostolic foundation. The Church is by this establishment and foundation arranged in a hierarchy of classes: the brothers and sisters as a whole, virgins and ascetics, martyrs and confessors, and the clergy headed

---

[15] Von Campenhausen.

by the bishop who sets the standard. His ideal bishop demands from the congregation virtue, execution of his commands, and submission to God's will, and in turn strengthens its faith, discipline, and righteousness. Cyprian insists that it is the correctness of the mode of election and of the ordination that makes a man truly a priest or bishop. He also reserves to the bishops of a province, and not to the local congregation or clergy, the competence to proceed against an unfaithful shepherd. For Cyprian, without the office of bishop the Church does not exist; and if the Church is not our mother, then God cannot be our father.

Cyprian's understanding of the role of bishop had substantial impact when the Church came to grasp the office of bishop in juridical terms several centuries later. His own practice somewhat tempers how his theory might at first blush be interpreted. For instance, he did consult his clergy and congregation for advice on whether to withhold absolution from those who had lapsed into heresy. He also apologized once for ordaining a subdeacon and a lector without the express consent of his clergy.

Cyprian was not alone in ascribing a privileged status to the bishop. About the same time, the Syriac *Didascalia* exhorts Christians to "love the bishop as a father, fear him as a king, honor him as a god." The *Didascalia* further stresses the rights and jurisdiction of the episcopal office and relegates the laity to a subordinate status. It also affirms that the Spirit of God dwells in the bishop who communicates it to others by the laying on of hands in baptism.[16]

The third century bears witness to two tasks of the bishop which seem to be of more ancient origin, but for which clear documentation exists only from the third. First, the church of Rome in 251 was supporting from the common purse the bishop, 64 presbyters, 7 deacons, 7 subdeacons, 42 acolytes, 52 exorcists, readers, and doorkeepers, and also 1,500 widows and needy. Thus the poor, especially the widows and orphans of the assembly, had become a special responsibility of the bishop. Secondly, several local churches had interpreted Paul's dictum against Christians' taking their fellows into the secular courts (1 Cor 6:1-6) to imply that local churches should have their own courts. Apparently bishops in the company of their clergy met beginning on Mondays with Christians who brought complaints against another member of the assembly. The goal of these courts seems to have been to arrange an agreement among the disputants before the whole church gathered again for Eucharist the next Sunday.[17]

By the end of the fifth century the bishop had become an official who had authority over all the Christians in his sector as well as being endowed

---

[16] Eno, "Shared Responsibility," 20, and von Campenhausen, 268–84.

[17] Henry Chadwick, "The Role of the Christian Bishop," 5–14.

with the duty and privilege of performing in person or through one of the priests delegated by him all the necessary sacramental functions. The bishop thus became a ruler over his diocese, and the liturgy became something done by the clergy for the laity. This development set the clergy as a class apart and was reinforced in the following century when the clergy began to wear a special costume and adopted a special rule of life based on the regulations for the Levites in the Old Testament. All this change seemed to occur without extensive opposition. Although special clerical dress was for a time forbidden.[18]

The Edict of Toleration and the Universal Church

The whole existence of the Church was transformed irrevocably in the fourth century by Constantine's edict of toleration. The Church changed abruptly from an illegal, secret society into the directing conscience of the empire. But Constantine's edict could not have come at a worse time for the Church. Only ten years earlier Diocletian had launched probably the most thorough and devastating persecution in the history of the Church, leaving much of its leadership either dead or in disarray. At an African synod of 305 only two of the bishops present were not compromised in some sense; one of their number was a double murderer. As a result of the persecution neophytes were often elected to the episcopacy, and catechumens were baptized, ordained, and consecrated in short order. Further, the Church brought to its task little or no organization above the local church level where, for almost three centuries, custom and tradition, conceived of as immemorial and enforced by ceaseless pressure from an alien world, had served as its guides.

Accorded freedom and respectability, the Church thrust itself into the charge given it by Constantine to act as the agent of imperial moral reform and deal with the unprecedented numbers of people who now wanted to become Christians. The mission of reforming the empire required that the Church be of one mind and be able to enforce that mind. This led to an increasing use of synods and councils (about which more later) where bishops could define collectively the articles of faith and judge what customs

[18] Besides the already mentioned sources, the following were helpful in compiling this section: Henry Chadwick, "The Circle and the Ellipse: Rival Concepts of Authority in the Early Church," *Jerusalem and Rome,* with Hans von Campenhausen (Philadelphia: Fortress, 1966) 23–36; Yves Congar, *Tradition and Traditions* and Robert Eno, *Teaching Authority in the Early Church* (Wilmington, Del.: Michael Glazier, 1984). The latter two were of assistance for the remaining sections of this chapter.

of the local churches needed to be modified. In this manner bishops evolved from conveyors of local church tradition into theological disputants and defenders of doctrine hammered out at synods and councils. For its own political purposes the empire was only too happy to encourage the episcopate in the direction of uniform belief, worship, and daily religious life. The increasing numbers of adherents required regional reorganization of the local churches. Certain apostolic churches had always possessed a certain prominence in their provinces, for example, Alexandria in Egypt, Antioch in Syria, and Rome in Italy. Other local churches of the province had submitted their local disputes to the apostolic Church for resolution and had tolerated a certain amount of intervention by the apostolic Church in their internal affairs. Later, in the fifth century, these three churches were joined by Jerusalem and Constantinople in a metropolitan system so that there emerged a hierarchy among churches of each region. The ecumenical council of Nicea first canonized this superstructure.[19]

During the fourth century the election of the bishop by acclamation of the people became a formality even though there are instances of rejection of bishops in this and the next century. Ideally, the bishop emerged from a process in which he was chosen by the local clergy after consultation with the nobility, then approved by the people, and finally consecrated by at least three of the neighboring bishops. In actual fact the elective power of the people was mostly negative: they could reject a candidate deemed unsuitable or settle disputes among the clergy when they offered more than one potential bishop. Nonetheless, in the early Church, more open, public competition existed for its top leadership as well as more participation by the people than any other institution in the empire.[20]

By the end of the fourth century Augustine stressed the importance of a consensus with antiquity in the Church, beyond the evident consensus of the contemporary universal Church. His slightly junior contemporary, Theodoret of Cyrus, spoke of the growing importance of earlier ecclesiastical writers as authorities in guiding the authentic interpretation of the faith, the beginnings of the imputation of authority to the Fathers of the Church.

To complete consideration of the bishop in the first millennium we might jump ahead to significant developments in relations between Rome and Germany during the ninth century. From the sixth century onward the Germans had been catechized and converted by missionaries commissioned by Rome. Progressively educated people adopted the Latin culture and welcomed the mass in Latin. Since Latin was unintelligible to the less educated, the majority in Germany was reduced to the status of bystanders at

---

[19] Dix.

[20] Chadwick, "The Role of the Christian Bishop," and Lynch.

the Mass and the already noted clericalization of the liturgy took on a pronounced character. The higher clergy there modeled themselves on the military landed aristocracy of feudalism and were rewarded with immense political power. The office of bishop became increasingly a matter of title by birth as aristocratic families sought to have relatives elected or appointed to episcopal office. In this situation Christian obedience was connected with juridical competence, especially in reference to appellate recourse, and salvation was tied to church order. The Rome-Germany pattern of influence, however, was not unilateral. The adoption of the Mainz Pontifical at Rome proves otherwise. The tradition of instruments during the ceremony of ordination introduced by that book serves as an example of a tendency in the Church to take over secular rituals as models for investing ecclesiastical officials with the symbols of their office.[21]

Not all authority in the early Church was clerical. In Africa especially, but elsewhere as well, from the third century onward martyrs who suffered for Christ were deemed to have imitated him most perfectly. If they died, they went straight to heaven. If they survived imprisonment and torture they were endowed with special gifts—for instance, for the forgiveness of sinners. If elected to church office they were frequently exempted from ordination in the usual manner although not from the ordination ceremony for a bishop. After the turmoil created by Montanism in the second century, there remained a profound mistrust of religious enthusiasm, ecstatic prophecy, and the claims for holiness. Yet holiness continued to be respected in the Church both as a source of authority and a prerequisite for election to orders. The Anchorite monks, a movement of lay spirituality, were held in very high esteem, as Athanasius' *Life of St. Anthony* testifies. Many monks were cajoled and occasionally coerced into becoming bishops in the fourth century and later. If the spiritual welfare of the people was to be a pastoral concern, the candidate for bishop had to be a holy man. That this conviction was widely shared emerges from *The Life of Martin of Tours* by Sulpicius Severus where a contrast is drawn between the bishops taken from the Roman aristocracy and the new clergy drawn from monks and ascetics.[22]

The development of authority among the ancient churches was not uniform; in fact, there were some broad differences between the East and the West. In the East the local churches thought of themselves as a Mystical Body of believers in fellowship with Christ through incorporation into him. To be saved meant to be deified: Christ became a human being that we might become godlike. This godlike character consisted in a new vision

---

[21] Edward Kilmartin, "Reception in History: An Ecclesiological Phenomenon and its Significance," *Journal of Ecumenical Studies* 21 (1989) 34–54.

[22] Eno, *Teaching Authority in the Early Church*, VI.

of life, a purification of the whole person which recapitulated what had gone before. The deified person was a king or queen, ruling over all of his or her faculties. Eastern Christians understood "the kingdom of God is in your midst" in this manner. Reform meant a return both upwards toward heaven and backwards in creation. In the reformed person the image of God that Adam and Eve possessed before their sin was restored. Innovation was generally regarded with suspicion since it was considered to be by necessity in the direction of the less good. As a result monasticism in the East tended to be eremitic, a retreat from the wicked world into which the sons and daughters of Adam and Eve had fallen. Away from the world, the holy monk contemplated heavenly things.

The circulation of decretals throughout the East constituted a quite complex process. Latin decretals, for instance, required translation into Greek, Syriac, and Coptic plus approval by the emperor, patriarch, and local bishop before they acquired a permanent abode. As a consequence, only the decretals of Chalcedon were kept everywhere. In the East doctrinal disputes were only settled when the proposed solution attained a consensus of the five patriarchates and reception by a majority of the local churches. A general council emerged as the paradigm of this process of consensus and reception. In this context the emperor of Byzantium possessed broad religious powers and duties. He could appoint bishops upon whom he conferred imperial insignia. He invoked and approved the early great councils whose decrees he enforced among his subjects.

In the West the Church was a two-tiered reality composed of the saints in heaven and the pilgrims on earth. These pilgrims concerned themselves especially with criteria of membership. Cyprian proposed his famous dictum, "Outside the Church, no salvation," as a principle for justifying the nonvalidity and nonefficaciousness of sacramental actions by ministers who had separated themselves from the true Church. The dictum, however, illustrates the penchant in Africa and later in Europe for determining who is a Christian in terms of membership in an earthly institution (a conviction also to be noted in Ignatius of Antioch and Origen).

This conviction that Jesus Christ had somehow effectively permeated the earthly (at least, the earthly that had become the Church) led Western Christians to see progress on earth as a genuine possibility. Early on Tertullian articulated this conviction well when he wrote of "reforming for the better." As a result, monks in the West tended to be apostolic, laboring to build up the body of Christ here and now.

In the West, not just Church but also higher civil officials understood Latin. This enabled Roman decretals (Rome had been an assiduous record keeper since the fourth century) to gain widespread esteem as sources of

Christian rightness. In the West, Rome was the unique apostolic Church. Its reputation as the only patriarchate to have preserved the apostolic faith without taint of error meant its traditions became normative for other local churches. This made it possible for the Bishop of Rome often to impose consensus on many Western local churches, though not so often as several popes would have liked. As a certainly earthly reality, Western churches saw themselves as separate from the empire and claimed a superiority of the clerical over the civil. The emperor was expected to be a defender of the faith, an enforcer of church decisions in the secular sphere, and someone charged to provide material sustenance for the church.[23]

The Emergence of Church Councils

The bishops of Asia Minor began meeting in groups midway through the second century to discuss collective action against the Montanists. Toward the end of the same century bishops from several regions of the East met to settle upon a single date for Easter (or so Eusebius tells us). For this reason Tertullian described councils as an Eastern practice. By the midpoint of the next century his own church, however, had adopted the same practice. During the persecution of Decius (250) a number of Christians in Africa, including several bishops and priests, had rendered sacrifice to the pagan gods or, at least, procured a certificate that they had done so. The corruption of so many bishops constituted a scandal of enormous proportions: who could be counted as having preserved the faith? Cyprian proposed that, while individual bishops had erred, the episcopacy as a whole had remained faithful and that they could best express the significance of fidelity for the one true faith by gathering in councils, which they frequently did at his insistence. In 268 a number of Eastern bishops gathered at Antioch to condemn Paul of Samosata for his trinitarian views. In 314 the emperor convoked a meeting of mostly Western and African bishops at Arles to deal with the Donatists.[24]

The freedom which the Church gained after 313 was particularly welcome to heretics. In the fourth century heresies could no longer be contained as local church affairs. For instance, Arius, a priest from the outskirts of Alexandria, soon embroiled the churches of Asia Minor and eventually most of the churches in the West in his doctrinal dispute with the bishops of Alexandria. Pelagius began in Rome, but Pelagianism became a serious

---

[23] Gerhart Ladner, *The Idea of Reform: Its Impact on Christian Thought and Action in the Age of the Fathers* (Cambridge: Harvard University Press, 1959).

[24] John Lynch, "The Magistery and Theologians from the Apostolic Fathers to the Gregorian Reform," *Chicago Studies* 17 (1978) 188–209.

concern in the churches of Africa and Jerusalem. There arose a need for councils of broad ecclesial representation that could achieve a consensus of faith and propose common courses of action. The implementation of conciliar decrees would, of course, be left to the local churches. Because religious agreement was so necessary for imperial peace the emperors were only too happy to accede to the petitions of clergy to convoke such councils, provide transport to the meeting place for the attending bishops, and corroborate and enforce the decrees in the empire.

Constantine convoked the first of these truly general councils at Nicea in 325 to settle the Arian dispute, the date of Easter, and some other Church matters. Its settlement of the question regarding Arius provoked considerable opposition since it used the word *homoousios* which was not a scriptural term; its use by Paul of Samosata had been condemned in the previous century at Antioch.[25] It required roughly a hundred years for Nicea to be accepted everywhere. The opposition was so vigorous that seemingly general councils of the West (Arimimium) and of the East (Seleucia) met in 359 and acceded to the wishes of Constantius II that Arius, or at least semi-Arianism, be rehabilitated. This turn of events provoked Ambrose's famous comment that the whole Church awoke to find itself Arian. A second now-called ecumenical council convened at Constantinople in 381 with no Westerners in attendance. For that reason this council was long viewed with suspicion in the West. In 451 the fourth ecumenical and great christological council of Chalcedon gathered. Its doctrine was not accepted in Egypt, Palestine, and Syria. Leo I, Bishop of Rome, received it selectively, approving only its doctrinal decisions. Constantinople II assembled in 553. The Bishop of Rome at the time, Vigilius, rejected its decisions though his successors eventually gave their approval. Leo II followed the precedent set by his more famous namesake and restricted his approval of Constantinople III (681) to its doctrinal canons and asked the Spanish bishops to do likewise, which they did at Toledo XIV.

Until proven otherwise, such assemblies were assumed to be marked by the presence of the Holy Spirit. The bishops gathered at such councils seem to have shared at least three assumptions: (1) conciliar gatherings presumed themselves to be authoritative as mediators of the faith of both the apostolic tradition and their own local churches; (2) they also looked for and expected reception of their decrees on the part of the universal Church; finally (3) they saw themselves as unconditionally bound to the Scriptures as faithfully transmitted in their preaching and that of their predecessors.

---

[25] Commonly the term is translated "consubstantial." I agree with Prestige that the Nicean usage is not technical and is better translated as "of the same stuff."

Reception of council teaching in the early Church was a long and complex process whereby local churches came to accept decisions by local or ecumenical councils. In the case of local decisions, each church presumed that any local church was truly a church and, therefore, could speak of the faith to its sister churches. In the case of the ecumenical conciliar decisions, churches assumed that the collectivity of bishops had uttered statements that might make a real difference in the faith of the local churches, even to the extent of requiring new creedal formulations. Such a claim, however, needed to be thoroughly tested. The testing process was twofold. Did the conciliar definitions represent a consensus of the whole Church at the time? This question would be answered in the affirmative if a virtual unanimity of the local churches received the definition as congruent with their faith. Could it be demonstrated that the conciliar definitions corresponded to the Scriptures and the tradition? The resolution of this issue was the more important in the process of reception.[26]

In concluding this survey of early conciliar development we should note that Sardica (343), Rimini (359), Ephesus (359), and Constantinople (754) were convoked and understood by their participants as ecumenical, but were not received as such in the universal Church.[27]

Petrine Primacy

The primacy in leadership of the Bishop of Rome emerged gradually over the first millennium. In the beginning Jerusalem constituted the center of Christianity as Paul's collections for the saints in Jerusalem and the first fifteen chapters of Acts show. After the destructions of the Holy City in 70 and 135 this centrality eventually passed to Rome, although there were regional differences. In the East, Rome was considered one of the five great patriarchates and respected as the one that had the best record for conserving the faith. African churches generally acknowledged that local and even regional decisions could be appealed to Rome and were final if ratified there. In the West, Rome functioned as the lone link with the apostles, especially after Antioch, Jerusalem, and Alexandria fell under Muslim control. Rome's word was never absolutely final in Western Europe,

---

[26] Kilmartin and Thomas Rausch, "Reception Past and Present," *Theological Studies* 47 (1986) 497–508.

[27] Besides the sources already cited, I want to acknowledge two articles by Robert Eno that were especially helpful in understanding how ecumenical councils came to be: "Authority and Conflict in the Early Church," *Eglise et Théologie* 7 (1976) 41–60, and "Pope and Council: The Patristic Origins," *Science et Esprit* 28 (1976) 183–211.

but its local tradition was deemed the sole and best guide for remaining in touch with the faith of the apostles.

In the year 96 Clement wrote a letter to Corinth in the name of the Roman church protesting the Corinthians' ouster of their presbyters and demanding the restoration of the presbyters to their rightful status. Sixteen years later Ignatius of Antioch referred to the church of Rome as "preeminent in love." Both Marcion and Montanus came to Rome to appeal their condemnations by local churches of the East. When Rome denied their appeals, their causes seem to have been lost. On the other hand, when Victor of Rome in 190 tried to impose the date on which Easter was celebrated at Rome on the churches of Asia Minor his interference met with stiff opposition. A decade earlier Irenaeus, noting that Rome was the only church of apostolic origin in the West, offered a list of bishops there that could be traced back to the foundation of the Church by Peter and Paul. The purpose of his list seems to have been to show that orthodox communion with Christ was present in Rome because a public succession of bishops of that church in faith assured the identity of the gospel preached by Peter and Paul with the present proclamation. Irenaeus' mention of Peter is not that usual in the second century. Elsewhere Peter's name appears only in *1* and *2 Clement,* Ignatius of Antioch, and Justin's *Dialogue with Trypho.*

Rome is first mentioned as the see of Peter at the beginning of the third century. In 250 Stephen of Rome and Cyprian of Carthage were involved in a hot dispute when the former tried to impose the Roman custom of not rebaptizing heretics or people baptized by heretics. In this dispute it becomes very clear that relations between Rome and other churches are asymmetrical. Other churches seldom attempted to impose their local customs on others; Roman bishops did so, at least in instances they regarded as greatly dangerous to the faith. Later Rome even tried to depose local bishops. By the end of the third century the Roman reputation for being right in the Lord was solidly entrenched: it had made the correct decision on heretics like Marcion and Montanus, the date of Easter, opposition to rebaptizing, and the practice of penance. Outside of Rome this "being right" did not come as a great surprise; the great apostles Peter and Paul had been martyred in Rome and undoubtedly exercised constant watch over the Roman church.

In 325 Nicea recognized the regional authority of the Roman patriarch.[28] In 340 this recognition came under question when Julius, then Bishop of Rome, readmitted to communion with himself some bishops

---

[28] James McCue, "The Beginnings through Nicea," *Papal Primacy and the Universal Church,* eds. Paul Empie and Austin Murphy (Minneapolis: Augsburg, 1974) 44–72.

who had been excommunicated by Eastern councils. Since the actions against these bishops had not been without substantial reasons, Julius' counter action shocked Eastern churches that had come to rely on Rome's steadfastness in the faith.

Damasus, who ruled the Roman church from 366 to 384, made the first clear claim to Peter as the foundation of his office. His successor, Siricius, sent a letter to Bishop Himerius of Terragona in 385 attempting to establish a uniform code of discipline over all the West and asserted that Peter lives on in each pope through whom he continues to direct the Roman church.[29]

Innocent I (401–17) claimed that the authentic tradition was given by St. Peter to the Roman church. In a letter to Bishop Decentius of Gubbio in 416 he asserted that all Western churches had been founded by Rome, and that the apostles had determined liturgical rituals in all their details and Rome had preserved these without change. He counseled conformity to the Roman, that is, apostolic ritual. His successor, Zosimus, wrote to Bishop Aurelius of Carthage that no one can reverse or reconsider a Roman decision. Aurelius waited until 424 to write to Celestine, then Bishop of Rome, protesting in his own name and that of the Council of Carthage the dispatching of a papal legate to intervene in the council's deliberations about a certain priest, Apiarius. It is in this context that Augustine's remark, *Causa finita est* [the case is finished], ought to be read; Augustine had made the remark after condemnations of Pelagianism at two earlier African councils were upheld by Rome.

The previous century of assertiveness on the part of bishops of Rome reached its apogee and was synthesized by Leo the Great (440–61). He taught that supreme authority in the Church was given by Christ to Peter, a commission that would perdure as long as Peter's confession remained true. The apostle Peter became the first Bishop of Rome, and, Leo declared, his authority has been perpetuated in his successors. Even now Peter is mystically present in the Roman See as head and source. As he is its source, all authority in the Church comes to others through Peter. The Bishop of Rome is distinguished from his brother bishops in that he possesses the fullness of power. As a result the hierarchic order of bishops and metropolitans culminates in the successor of Peter. Innocent, Zosimus, Celestine, and Leo all claimed the controversial right to intervene in Africa. Near the end of the fifth century another strong pope, Gelasius, observed that the universal acceptance of the Roman rejection of canon 28 of Chalcedon showed that Rome was the sole and final arbiter in the Church

---

[29] Chadwick, "The Circle and the Ellipse."

regarding discipline and doctrine. Furthermore, Gelasius held that God will never allow the Roman church to fall into error, adding that the universal Church is a hierarchy bound together by Rome's ultimate authority. As if to prove his point he added the papal decretals to the synodal collection of canons. He also concurred in the general Western conviction that spiritual power is separate from, but superior to, temporal authority.

The one obvious break in this tradition of popes' asserting their prerogatives appeared in the person of Gregory the Great (590–604). He styled himself "the servant of the servants of God" and argued that the cohesive element in the Church was humility. He conducted himself toward the Eastern churches in a collegial rather than monarchical manner and asserted that the true faith emerged from a consensus of the five patriarchates. His zeal led him to commission a number of missionaries to the lands of northern Europe, thereby creating churches there which were fiercely loyal to the founding church of Rome.

A century later the belief that Rome had never fallen into error despite the lapses of all the other great apostolic churches was firmly fixed in the West. By the middle of the seventh century the Roman creed was the norm of true faith. In 649 the *Liber Dominus* of the Lateran Synod declared that the Bishop of Rome was universal pope and supreme arbiter. In 858 Nicholas I declared Rome the font of tradition for the whole Church and claimed that the power of Rome to judge bishops came from Christ himself. For Nicholas the Church was essentially a clerical community. The apostolic teaching had been integrally preserved in the Roman church whose judgments were irreversible and unreviewable. This papal supremacy precluded secular intervention in church affairs.[30]

In the ninth century the scholar Alcuin disputed that orthodoxy was simply a matter of submitting to Roman preaching. Orthodoxy was found in the Scriptures and the faith confession of the universal Church. The sanction of the Roman church and the approval by the universal Church constitute coordinate tests of orthodoxy. The aforesaid universality is discovered by a careful collation of scriptural and canonical sources and the establishment of a consensus among the Fathers.

In the same century the False Decretals of Isidore appeared. They also affirmed that true faith was attained through obedience of lower to the higher. The Church was a priesthood hierarchically ordered. The decretals insisted that all bishops shared in the Petrine commission (shades of

---

[30]   Robert Eno, "Some Elements in the Pre-History of Papal Infallibility," *Teaching Authority and Infallibility in the Church,* eds., Paul Empie, Austin Murphy, and Joseph Burgess (Minneapolis: Augsburg, 1978) 238–58.

Cyprian), but conceded Roman jurisdiction was supreme, so much so that only Rome had the power to call synods.[31]

Conclusion

Any examination of the first thousand years of the Church's existence reveals some sharp contrasts with the Church today. For instance one finds precious little reflection on the nature of the Church itself. What the primitive and early Christians thought the Church was must be gleaned from what is implied about the Church in what is directly said on other topics, for example, christology. Also, one finds little deliberation on Church authority itself. Here the behavior of people in the Church provides some clues into how Church authority was conceived. Finally, the present preoccupations with juridical issues receive far less attention. The turn towards juridicism began with a number of popes, especially Gregory VII, in the eleventh century. Ecclesiology, the reflection of the Church on its own nature, is a post-Reformation phenomenon. Concern with the meaning of ecclesiastical authority became a focal issue in theology over the last two centuries. Thus, we must now turn our attention to the next millennium of the Church's history to complete our study of ecclesiastical authority.

[31] Karl Morrison, *Tradition and Authority in the Western Church 300–1140* (Princeton, N.J.: Princeton University Press, 1969), and George Tavard, "The Papacy in the Middle Ages," *Papal Primacy and the Universal Church,* 98–104.

CHAPTER 5

The Second Millennium

Medieval Christendom:
Ecclesial Autonomy and the Juridical Turn

At the beginning of the eleventh century educated people lived in and of the Bible. The Scriptures, however, needed to be read in the light of what was written in the book of the world and the human soul, and the full significance of the last two was available only in the light of the Bible. The world, humanity, and the communion of saints formed one harmonious whole; all were the work of the same divine wisdom; all belonged to a hierarchical order with the Scriptures as divine revelation at its summit. The educated sought to express this magnificent and intricate order in a single work—an effort which culminated in the Gothic cathedrals and theological summas. In these works all of creation came to be regulated according to the sacred text.

For all medievals there existed one overarching and absolute authority, the creator God who bestowed the gift of being on all creatures, allowing them to become expressions of his truth and goodness, thereby becoming authorities in their own right. Only the Scriptures, where God had been revealed to the prophets and apostles, possessed the absolute guarantee of first truth. In the Scriptures human cooperation was present, but totally subordinated to God. Another inferior but no less important communication of truth by God consisted in the world of creation, especially where that world became Church. There the divine authority was bestowed on the *majores,* the heads and teachers of the Church, especially the Fathers, ecumenical councils and more important synods, and popes. But this authority also reached to lesser authorities such as the masters of sacred doctrine in the schools. While what the greater or lesser authorities said was not absolute in the way the Scriptures were, their teaching did genuinely participate in the authority of God which, for present authorities, could be demonstrated by ecclesial approval and conformity to ancient Church teaching. All these authorities were, of course, dependent on the Holy Spirit.

In their conception of authority the medievals differed from their forebears of the first millennium in two important ways. First, they definitely believed that creatures by their very creaturehood could express God's very truth. The ancients were more suspicious. For them the world had been profoundly corrupted by Adam's sin, and most of it now lay outside the grasp of the divine will. Only where grace abounded in the saints of the Church (on earth and in heaven) could people speak confidently of a participation in God's truth. As a result, when thoughtful ancient Christians confronted the obvious wisdom of Greek philosophy they argued that the source of that wisdom lay in the Old Testament. Thus the medieval mind was distinguished by its incipient conviction that all creatures express God's truth. Secondly, during the Middle Ages a subtle shift took place in how church members viewed the teaching of the Church. In the first millennium people focused on the content of what was said and looked for a continuity between that content and the tradition of the Church. Furthermore, that focus on continuity sought a connection between a local church here and now and apostolic origins. Even when the Church as a whole came to accept the great ecumenical councils, the process involved reception of the faith of the councils by local churches. The medievals, on the other hand, cast their attention more on the teacher than the teaching and on authorities who could express the faith of the whole Church, that is, popes and councils or the unanimous consent of the Fathers.[1]

The above shifts had profound consequences for the understanding of ecclesiastical authority. First of all, medievals saw the cohesive element within the Church as its visible, administrative order, not its mystical union with Christ or the gifts received from the Holy Spirit for the good of the whole body. Secondly, governmental authority, including the government of the Church, derived from the consent of at least the articulate governed (generally those able to be so because of inherited social status). As a result, both the ruler's assumption of office and the validity of his official acts depended on approval or at least tacit acceptance by his more powerful subjects. Numerous medieval popes disputed the full force of this dependence in regard to the papal office, but even they based their counterclaim on agreement with their predecessors seen as witnesses in a line of succession rather than as participants in the same faith. Finally, in the eleventh century everyone was concerned about the sad state of the Church and

---

[1] Yves Congar, *Tradition and Traditions,* 86–101.

agreed that the troubles stemmed from illicit changes in Church custom. A widespread discrepancy existed between the eleventh-century Church and the Church of the apostles, martyrs, and Fathers.

The troubles were simony, the selling of Church offices to their occupants, and lay investiture. Technically, lay investiture referred to the fact that a newly elected abbot or bishop received his ring and staff from the prince, king, or emperor before his installation or consecration. The real problem lay in the fact that through lay investiture secular authorities manifested the nearly total control they exercised over the appointment of Church authorities and the exercise of their office. Monasteries, for instance, had frequently been founded and enriched by local princes or great nobles who expected political and economic support in return. The loyalty of the local bishop and the securing of the election of an appropriately loyal candidate generally formed the cornerstone of an astute feudal lord's policy.

The tone of the Church's assault on simony and lay investiture was set by a group of particularly capable and assertive popes, beginning with the accession of Leo IX in 1049 and ending with the death of Gregory VII in the year 1085. Their impact on the exercise of Church authority was decisive for the remainder of the present millennium. They all strove to deliver the Church from lay control.

These popes were aided by the fact that Rome was the only local church in the West of apostolic origin and the widespread belief that the Apostolic See had always preserved the faith intact. On this basis the popes from 1049 to 1085 argued that only Rome could distinguish between contemporary error and ancient truth, suspend the force of Church canons in cases of need, and promulgate new laws to meet unprecedented necessities. In general, their view of reform was that correction of abuses at the local level would take place when the local church was brought into congruence with the ancient order of the Roman church. Within this perspective, diversities of place were not acknowledged as legitimate; instead, they were seen as conducive to schism, and to be replaced by Roman custom. Necessity, however, did permit bishops of Rome to add to the body of Roman law by decretal. They did so because they exercised their authority in a long line of succession going back to Peter. So their decrees along with those of their predecessors were normative among legal sources, and the canonicity of any custom or text depended on its concordance with or explicit approval by Rome.

For these popes, the Church on earth was a Church militant in which every Christian could be enlisted as a soldier of Christ in the struggle against simoniac ordinations and lay control. In this struggle the priesthood from the pope down to the last priest or cleric would play a leading role since ideally the priesthood should be motivated by spiritual and not temporal interests. The reform envisioned episcopal elections followed by consecrations with no intervening obeisance to lay rulers. Thus, leadership in the Church would be totally under the control of the priesthood. Then, it was reasoned, the Holy Spirit could operate freely and the men elected would be ordained for spiritual ends.

The popes from Leo through Gregory were not solely preoccupied with ideals. They saw, for instance, that too many priests and bishops were consumed with familial interests, the economic aggrandizement of their churches, and the completion of the political tasks allotted to them by their respective lords. Only Roman control would insure that genuine reform of the Church would ensue at the local level. For example, these popes cut through the knotty conundrum created by the ordination of men who obtained their election through simony and the long-standing tradition in the West that even unworthy ordinations were valid by decreeing that simoniac ordinations and consecrations were legitimate only if the recipients submitted to papal authority.

In their zeal to reform, these popes had an exemplar in the monastic reform of Cluny. Gregory VII had been a monk at Cluny from 1047 to 1049 and came to Rome in 1050 where he became an advisor to popes until his own election in 1073. These popes realized that the core of Cluny's reform lay in its spirituality, with liturgy at the center. It did not escape their notice that the Cluniac monasteries had an exempt status: that is, they were exempt from local control which linked them more closely to the pope than to local church authorities. Thus, all these popes sought a reform grounded in and guaranteed by the Church's spiritual essence incorporated in its priesthood, to which both liturgy and doctrine have been specially entrusted. This priesthood was, in its very institution by Christ, constituted with the Bishop of Rome as its head.[2]

Besides the strong reassertion and extension of papal primacy, these popes also tried to set the universal Church on a solid canonical foundation. They conceived the Church as theonomy, an autonomous and sovereign system of rights in law which expressed a superior divine law. They attached enormous importance to the formal validity of ecclesiastical authority, the possession of a title in Church law. They stressed the legal relevance of the canons (records) of the Roman church and emphasized the degrees of responsibility imposed on each rank in the Church's hierarchy.

[2] Gerhard Ladner, "Reformation," *Ecumenical Dialogue at Harvard,* eds. Samuel Miller and Ernest Wright (Cambridge: Harvard University Press, 1964) 172–90.

In their view, bishops did possess genuine authority. They belonged to an order of teachers and at consecration had been entrusted with the Gospels. They likewise contributed to ecclesiastical law through the body of regulations they established singly in their dioceses, in letters or treatises, and collectively over a province in their synodal decrees. The norm for the rightness of these episcopal regulations was agreement with the canons of the Roman church. It is indicative of the juridical bent of the popes from Leo to Gregory that one looks in vain for a theological book like Leo the Great's *Tome* to the Council of Chalcedon or Gregory the Great's *Moralia*. These popes wrote letters or issued official documents.

Thus the pope was juridically supreme in the Church. Papal authority, by a positive divine institution, emanated directly from him as a font to the faithful and their bishops, the cardinals and even general councils, which had no power to restrict or augment papal authority. All the means of salvation were conveyed through the imperishable apostolate of St. Peter acting in the pope. Dissent from the Roman church was connected with heresy or idolatry.

Leo IX (1045–54) maintained that, because of Christ's commission to Peter, the Roman bishop became the supreme guardian of teaching and discipline in the Church. The authenticity of his interpretation of doctrine was displayed in the establishment of churches and the obedience which bound bishops to the pope as judges to their king. Peter Damian opined that the primacy of Peter continued in the Roman See, incarnated in the pope as safeguard of ecclesiastical truth and cohesion. Gregory VII (1073–85) boasted that the law of Roman pontiffs prevailed in more lands than the laws of the Roman emperor. In his *Dictatus Papae* (1075), a list of twenty-seven propositions, he made the first clear claim to a primacy of immediate jurisdiction touching every Christian. In it he claimed the power to dispense subjects from their oath of allegiance to the emperor and the right to appoint and dispense bishops. He asserted that papal decisions have force of law in the Church and that the Roman See is subject to the judgment of no one. All authority in the Church comes from the pope, and there exists everywhere the right of appeal to Rome. Here and elsewhere in his writings the crisis in the Church involves hierarchical institutions and reform is not reform of persons but of local churches and the Church as a whole. The general renewal of the Church will occur with the reestablishment of the primitive and glorious state of ecclesiastical holiness, which was the glory of the church of Rome. The required justice or righteousness consists in conformity to the faith of St. Peter and his successors because Christ had prayed that the faith of Peter should not fail so that he could confirm his brethren in the faith (Luke 22:22). Peter's justice is founded on the love of Christ.

Christians show their love for Christ by their love for, by their justice under, and their unity with the church of Rome.[3]

These reforming popes were assiduous administrators as well. They persuaded prelates in Spain to substitute the Roman Rite for their Visigoth liturgies. They all pressed clerical celibacy as a central component in the reform of the clergy. Gregory centralized the right to dispense, appointed a whole array of papal legates, and insisted that the pallium (a cloak symbolizing the power of archbishops) be bestowed in Rome.

Not all these moves, especially the promotion of clerical celibacy, met with broad approval. Peter Damian's attempt to enforce clerical celibacy in Milan provoked a popular uprising. The Roman clergy under Stephen IX pronounced clerical continence vain and frivolous. After the bishop of Brescia read Nicholas II's letter prohibiting the marriage of clergy, his priests beat him so badly that he almost died. For defending Gregory VII's prohibition of the same, an abbot was set upon at the Synod of Paris (1074) and the archbishop of Rouen was stoned by his clergy. Synods at Worms and Brixen condemned Gregory for all manner of things and declared him unfit for his office. In 1084 more than half the cardinals convened and elected Clement III, an antipope. The dissident cardinals accused Gregory of not consulting them and insisted that the powers of St. Peter reside not in the person of the pope but in the Roman See as embodied in the cardinalate, whom the pope represented only as long as the cardinals supported him. Gregory died in 1085 in exile. A widely read work, *De Unitate Ecclesiae Conservanda* (On Conserving the Unity of the Church, 1090–93), posthumously justified the cardinals' action, especially in relation to Gregory's disregard for the rightful privileges of local churches and his treatment of Henry IV.[4]

The influence of the popes of this period on the subsequent Church was profound. After them the Church in the West clearly had a magisterium. In the first millennium, the faith of the Church was embodied in what was taught as authenticated in the tradition. After Gregory the focus transposed itself to the teacher, and his authenticity depended on his being possessed of appropriate jurisdiction. The idea of the unity of the Church was transformed into uniformity of liturgical language, discipline, and creedal formulations. The moral behavior of Christians was hereafter to be primarily regulated by the legislative and judicial governance of Church officials (and not by the catechesis that comes in one's family, living together with other Christians, and the celebration of the Eucharist). The

[3] Congar, *Tradition and Traditions,* 135.
[4] Morrison, 294–312.

Church came more and more to be viewed as a sacerdotal hierarchy centered on the Bishop of Rome.

When the Church became a hierarchical structure set over and above the empire with the papacy at its summit, the assertions of the papacy paralleled the imperial claims in the field of law. The Bishop of Rome possessed a juridical and administrative headship which gave him juridical competence. That there were two parallel political orders in Christendom, one lay, the other clerical, was confirmed in the Concordat of Worms of 1122. Persistent and powerful resistance on the part of the Holy Roman emperors had not stemmed the tide of a papacy intent on turning the Church into a visible, institutional reality.

In the next century popes managed to reserve the term "Vicar of Christ" for themselves. Prior to that, the term applied to any priest who was understood to be a representative of a transcendental power. When "Vicar of Christ" came to apply only to the pope, the term meant the representation of a power given in the beginning by Christ to one who assumes Christ's place and hands his power on to those who come after him in a historical sequence of transmission and succession. In the earlier usage the focus was upon what God was doing in the priest; in the later, on the handing on by the recipient with God consigned to the role of originator of the whole process.

In 1130 a contested papal election occurred, and two men, Innocent II and Anacletus II who died in 1138, competed for the papacy. Eventually Lateran I settled the dispute, but not until it became obvious that both men had been elected by the clergy and people of Rome, each one was consecrated by cardinal bishops at an altar of St. Peter, and both had been enthroned in the Lateran. In other words, the traditional canonical elements had been satisfied in the case of each claimant. The ensuing arguments pro and con turned on the consent of the faithful. Who did orthodox Romans count as pope? The Eastern prelates? Kings and princes? Thus, the ancient rule of consensus became a political doctrine of assent.[5]

Challenges to Juridicism: Canonists, Friars, and Schoolmen

In the twelfth century, the canonists came to the fore. Gratian, their foremost example, legitimized the mutual independence of the spiritual and the temporal orders, though he supported the papal contention that the prince was subject to spiritual authority. For him the Holy See constituted the supreme arbiter in matters of faith, and all doctrinal disputes ought to be referred there for resolution. The decisions of the pope, however, were

---

[5] Morrison, 335.

to be accepted only if they were in evident accord with the tradition. For his fellow canonists, the Church was two things: it was the community of believers, a perfect society infused with and sustained by the Holy Spirit in an unfailing corporate life; the Church was also a system of clerical offices which derived their authority from above and outside the community. Each aspect of the Church spawned its own type of authority. Church leaders possessed sacramental and sacerdotal powers, especially the power to remit sins. These powers were absolute. The same leaders also had powers of jurisdiction, of which the power to impose penance and to excommunicate were paradigmatic. These powers were relative to the possessor. Priests could absolve and impose necessary sanctions in private confessions; bishops could govern in their dioceses; and the pope had the authority to bind all the faithful to his decisions. In the twelfth century, canonists generally agreed that the whole Church had been granted indefectibility, and that the pope was supreme arbiter concerning articles of faith and possessed juridical supremacy.[6]

By the end of the twelfth century, a movement began to surface promoting a profound evangelical spirit not always consonant with the centralizing tendencies of the previous century. The Franciscans, for example, insisted that the community's superior be a minister and a servant of the other friars and behave towards all as their lesser and inferior. In other words, Franciscan ideals of authority were at the outset decidedly evangelical. Furthermore, Francis preached a change of mind and heart that invited his hearers to a more personal (rather than institutional) Christian righteousness.[7] Not long after, the Dominicans prescribed a local chapter of faults daily, provincial chapters every Michelmas (September 29), and annual general chapters which, over the first 140 years of the order's existence, met in 52 different places all over Europe. That is, they provided a model whereby clerical superiors were compelled to seek consultation (and not only in Rome).[8]

In the thirteenth century another magisterium appeared, the magisterium of doctors of theology. The theological faculty of the University of Paris considered itself, and was generally recognized as, an authentic authority on the meaning of doctrine. Some spoke of three magisteria in the Church: the priesthood centered in Rome; the kingdom focused on the German emperor; and the academy with Paris as its center. A few even

---

[6] Brian Tierney, *Foundations of Conciliar Theory* (Cambridge: Harvard University Press, 1955).

[7] Ladner, "Reformation," 186–90.

[8] John McNeill, "The Relevance of Conciliarism," *Who Decides for the Church*, 81–112.

drew comparisons between the threefold magisteria and the three Persons of the Trinity. At first Church officials looked askance at this novelty, condemning schoolmen such as Berengarius on the Eucharist, Gilbert de la Poirée on the Trinity at Rheims (1148), Peter Lombard on christology at Tours (1163), and Joachim de Fiore on the Trinity at the ecumenical council of Lateran IV (1215). This last council, however, unwittingly enhanced the magisterium of the academy when it used the scholastic term *transubstantiation* as a key term in one of its decrees; later the Council of Vienne (1312), using another scholastic notion, spoke of the human soul as the form of the body. Florence (1438–45) published its Decree for the Armenians (1439), a rough paraphrase of Aquinas's *De articulis fidei et ecclesiae sacramentis*. These three instances enhanced the authority of the schoolmen as competent to judge the validity of papal opinions in the light of their congruence with the Scriptures, the Fathers of the Church, ecumenical councils, and earlier popes.[9]

In the aftermath of the election of the antipope at Rome, first the canonists and later the schoolmen began to question the unlimited powers several successive popes seemed to claim. This process of questioning eventually led to the almost unanimous thesis in the thirteenth century that a pope could lapse into heresy and, for that lapse, be deposed. Why? Because the special powers of the papacy belonged to the Holy See, and not to a particular pope as a person. Some theologians and many canonists accepted the contention of the dissident cardinals of 1084 that the Petrine power was conferred on the cardinalate as a body to whom the reigning pope was responsible for his actions. All agreed a pope had the power to revise disciplinary decrees of his predecessors, but insisted that every pope was bound by revelation as encapsulated in the dogmas defined by the Church. A pope who wavered and taught something contrary to the faith, acted against the welfare of the whole Church; as a result, his power was at the very least suspended in regard to that particular action or even lost entirely if he contumaciously persisted in his action. Most medieval theologians thought there had been at least one such heretical pope: Anastasius II (496–98). What agency was competent to determine whether a pope had taught a heretical opinion? Clearly the whole Church! But a consensus grew that the proper body to execute such a judgment was a general council.

The Supreme Pontiff and the Avignon Schism

The power of the papacy reached its apogee in the Middle Ages during the reign of Innocent III (1198–1215). He taught and acted upon the

[9] Yves Congar, "Theologians and the Magisterium in the West: From the Gregorian Reform to the Council of Trent," *Chicago Studies* 17 (1978) 214–17.

fullness of power of jurisdiction over the universal Church. On that basis he intervened widely in the affairs of local churches and maintained that his office was the source of all other authority in the Church. Over the next two centuries the prestige that Innocent took for granted was badly damaged by the dispute Boniface VIII had with Philip the Fair, resulting in the Avignon Schism.

In 1296 Philip decided to tax the clerics of France. When they appealed to Rome, Boniface defended their traditional exemption and later excommunicated Philip for continuing to tax the Church. Philip retaliated by circulating parodies of the bull of excommunication and persuading all the major theologians of Paris, except Duns Scotus, to support him in his argument with Boniface. On November 18, 1302, Boniface sought to put an end to the conflict when he issued a solemn bull, *Unam Sanctam,* usually remembered for its assertion that it is "necessary to the salvation of every human creature to be subject to the Roman Pontiff." He was particularly keen to defend two principal contentions of his predecessors: (1) that there were two distinct orders in Christendom, one priestly, the other lay; and (2) that the lay was subject to the priestly. Temporal power needed to be exercised within, for, and at the direction of the priesthood with the pope at its apex. According to Boniface complete independence of the temporal from the spiritual could be compared to a two-headed monster.

Within the Church Boniface was quite content to accept that papal authority, though essentially different from the episcopal order, remained within it and that the episcopate possessed universal jurisdiction as a body. Outside the ecclesiastical order, however, the pope's power was supreme; he had jurisdiction over kings and emperors. For Boniface creation constituted a visible hierarchy that participated in a celestial hierarchy. In creation the "Church represents one Mystical Body," that is, Christendom as the sum total of all Christian believers in both their spiritual and social relationships. The papacy sits at the summit of the created hierarchy with the pope as the visible head of the Mystical Body on earth, making visible in himself the invisible and mystical Lord Jesus in heaven. As a consequence, union with Christ means obedience to his vicar the pope.

Philip the Fair had no interest in Boniface's grandiose vision of creation and Christendom. He wanted a lay realm completely separate from the Church and a France free from subjection to a German emperor. In that sense he is the father of the modern secular state. In 1303 he dispatched mercenaries to kidnap Boniface and detain him at Anagni. An uproar followed in Italy, and Philip was forced to release Boniface who conveniently died some months later. In 1305 the French king secured the election of the archbishop of Bordeaux as Clement V and invited Clement to move the papacy to Avignon in southern France where it stayed until 1377. In that year Gregory XI acceded to widespread desires in the Church and returned to Rome where he died in March of the following year.

One Spanish, four Italian, and eleven French cardinals met in consistory and elected Urban VI on April 8, 1378. During the electoral process, they were torn by dissension within and surrounded by rioters outside. Urban soon proved willful and obnoxious to the cardinals. So, all the original electors save one who had died reconvened and elected Robert of Geneva as Clement VII. Clement immediately betook his papacy to Avignon while Urban maintained his in Rome. For the next thirty-seven years the Church had at least two popes until the Council of Constance settled the schism in 1415.[10]

The Problem of Unity and the Emergence of Conciliarism

The Avignon Schism provoked a crisis within the Church with prominent clerical and lay Christians ranged on both sides of the controversy. For Church canonists, two concurrently reigning popes raised the major problem: whence the unity of the Church? Since the competing popes regularly declared their rivals guilty of heresy, how was the Church to be protected from an erring pope, and where would people find the unfailing guidance and authority Christ had promised to his Church? The general response of the canonists to these questions was that the Church as the congregation of the faithful remained one in the faith and sacraments while its head fell into error. The visible cornerstone of ecclesial unity, then, was shifted from the papacy to the whole Church which was seen as the superior to the Holy See. The whole community now possessed the fullness of power. Matthew 28:18 (Christ's promise to be with the Church in perpetuity) applied to the universal Church and could not be applied to Rome because it was a local church. As canonistic thinking moved in the direction of conciliarism, one notes in both the conciliarist arguments and the counterarguments of papalist writers the absence of two earlier convictions: Christ cedes his place as head of the Mystical Body to be represented visibly in the pope or the body faithful. And the relationship between the Church and the Eucharist disappears as an overriding theme, replaced by concern over the relationship between the pope and the Church universal.

According to many canonists, popes were rightfully elected by cardinals acting in the name of the whole Church. When popes fell into heresy,

---

[10] George Tavard, "The Bull *Unam Sanctam* of Boniface VIII," *Papal Primacy and the Universal Church*, 105–18.

they could be deposed by a judgment of the whole Church; the best vehicle for expressing that judgment was a general council. Councils were assemblies where the Holy Spirit spoke through the elect to the whole Church, represented as fully as possible there. For this reason, a general council was the best path to reform in the schism. This solution drew upon assumptions shared by the strongest popes themselves. First of all, a pope surrounded by the other pastors of the Church in council had more authority than when he acted alone. Secondly, the articles of faith uttered by a general council were inviolable. Therefore, the pope as supreme judge in matters of faith, was required to judge according to the doctrinal canons of these councils and could not reject them. To this latter assumption the canonists added only the generally held legal principle: an equal could not bind an equal.[11]

Behind all the legal reflections of the canonists lay the medieval idea of a corporation. The Church is a corporation where power is shared by all the members. The pope can represent the corporate authority as an administrator of Church unity which requires a representation as universal as possible. But only the Holy Spirit fully encapsulates the unity of the corporation in its deepest sense. Most of the ecclesial application of theory on corporations concerned the office of local bishop. The bishop was the proctor of the local church. While he could freely conduct the ordinary day-to-day business of the diocese, he needed the cooperation and consent of his cathedral chapter in conferring benefices and privileges, alienating church property, or passing judgment on cases which affected the well-being of the whole corporation. The principle here was that no bishop had the right to dispose of church goods, material or spiritual, as his own property. Thus, the bishop as representative needed actual delegation from the community. Episcopal jurisdiction (which was called full power) derived from the bishop's election and not his consecration. If the bishop died and left the bishopric vacant, his jurisdiction devolved to his inferiors who elect (the cathedral chapter) and his sacramental powers to his superiors who consecrate (the neighboring bishops).

In canonistic theory, the idea of corporation as applicable to the bishop was extended to encompass the pope as head of the Church. The head together with the members of the corporation formed one body. An ecclesiastical head could not act without the consent of the members since, as head, the pope represents the community no longer as a personification (as the bishop represented the local community in the early Church) but by

---

[11] C.M.D. Crowder, "Introduction" to *Unity, Heresy, and Reform 1378–1460* (London: Edward Arnold, 1977) 1–40, and Francis Oakley, *Council Over Pope?* (N.Y.: Herder & Herder, 1969).

delegation, that is, by election, either explicit or tacit, of the sovereign community.[12]

Individual conciliarists did nuance these theories differently. The Dominican John of Paris agreed that authority in a corporation was not concentrated in its head, but diffused among all the members. Consequently, any prelate was the steward and not the lord of his church. Prelates hold all their powers, whether sacramental or jurisdictional, immediately from God; but jurisdiction is also conferred by the election and consent of the people. Bishops receive their jurisdiction not from the pope, but from the members of the local church. The papacy, which is from God and indestructible, is not the pope. The authority of the papacy is conferred directly by God, but the duly appointed electors for the Church decide which individual will hold that authority. The papacy becomes vacant whenever an individual pope forfeits the consent of the cardinal-electors or, more properly, is removed from office by a general council. General councils can so act whenever a pope utters heresy, exceeds his powers in pronouncing on heresy, commits a serious crime, or is proven incompetent in his administration. Peter received from Christ both orders, an indelible and supernatural gift from God which makes him one with the other apostles, and the primacy of jurisdiction which depends on human election and consent. Those who elect and consent can, on the same basis, depose. A pope once deposed is no longer pope, for it is precisely the primacy of jurisdiction which makes him pope.

The distinctive contention of the conciliarist Durantius was that all the bishops of the Church should convene in council every ten years to reform the Church. Thus, he suggested a general council should be a regular, and not an extraordinary, occurrence. Marsilius of Padua in his *Defensor pacis* contended that government in the Church belongs to the Catholic people as a whole which actualizes that authority in a general council representative of all parts of the Church. Henry of Langestein declared a council superior to the pope and reminded his readers that the universal Church could not err. Gerson along with John Major said that it was the inherent right of any community to judge its ruler.[13]

Innocent III had unwittingly contributed to incipient conciliarism when he decided to make Lateran IV more representative of Western Christendom. He invited so many abbots and priors that they far outnumbered the bishops present.[14] The council then mandated annual synods in dioceses

---

[12] Tierney, *Foundations of Conciliar Theory.*
[13] McNeill, "The Relevance of Conciliarism," 97–103.
[14] Ibid., 86.

and ecclesiastical provinces plus triennial chapters for religious orders. In 1409 a council at Pisa passed judgment on both Benedict XIII of Avignon, who was supported by the Spaniards and the Scots, and Gregory XIII of Rome, who had the support of Naples and Germany. The council declared both of them heretics and schismatics and deposed each one as unfit for office. It then elected a Franciscan, Peter Philargi, as Alexander V who died shortly thereafter. The council replaced Alexander with Baldessari Cossa, an able soldier and administrator, who took the name of John XXIII. For the next six years, Christendom had three popes.

John XXIII convoked the Council of Constance (1414–18) to restore obedience to one pope, suppress the heresies of John Hus, and undertake reform of the Church. When the council first met, without the Spanish in attendance, it seemed as if warring factions would never agree on a single pope. The whole assembly, however, did concur in a novel strategy: that the whole be broken down into "Four Nations" of England, France, Germany, and Italy. Eventually all four nations called for the resignations of Benedict, Gregory, and John. John tried to flee, but the emperor returned him to the council in chains. He graciously resigned. Gregory offered his resignation the next year, accepting a cardinal's hat for his good deed. In 1417 Benedict's staunch supporters, the absent Spanish, abandoned him, and the council confidently deposed him. It had already elected a successor to all three, Martin V.

Constance also issued two important documents. In *Frequens* it mandated the regular convocation of general councils by the pope. In another, more important decree, *Haec sancta,* Constance declared that a general council receives its power from Christ, and not the pope, and that every Christian including the pope could be judged in a council. This latter assertion is probably a subscription to the thesis that a pope can be heretical. Finally, *Haec sancta* taught that all Catholics must obey what general councils teach in matters of faith.[15]

The conciliarists did not roll over and die after Constance. They took over another council at Basel in 1433 and under the leadership of Gerson, rector of the University of Paris, issued *Dudum sacrum* which declared that a general council was superior to the pope. By the time the document was promulgated most of the bishops in attendance had departed, and *Dudum sacrum* was never received in the universal Church. The last antipope, Felix V, was elected in 1439.

One other attempt in the Middle Ages to restrict the power of the pope concerned the doctrine of papal infallibility. This doctrine was first proposed

---

[15] C.M.D. Crowder, "Introduction," 7–28.

by what history books now call the "spiritual" Franciscans anxious to restrict the power of Pope John XXII and to bind him to the decrees regarding their order issued by a number of papal predecessors. He would be so bound if these decrees were regarded as irreformable. The immediate occasion for their making this claim was the revocation by John in 1322 of Nicholas III's Bull *Exiit* of 1275, which had regulated Franciscan life for over forty years. The spiritual Franciscans responded the following year that *Exiit* was intrinsically irreformable and, along with a similarly infallible bull of Gregory IX in 1231, had defined the absolute poverty of Christ and Franciscan poverty as the abandonment of worldly goods, whether held singly or in common. For John both bulls were disciplinary decrees, and he resented the imputation of infallibility to them. He maintained his own freedom to revoke the bulls and saw the spirituals as undisciplined troublemakers.

They turned to a *Quaestio* of Peter John Olivi, O.F.M., which identified Francis of Assisi with the angel who is sent by God to open the sixth seal in the Apocalypse. This veil limited people to a literal interpretation of the Scriptures and prevented a spiritual interpretation which would reveal the true meaning of the gospel. Francis, therefore, had inaugurated a new era of world history which would culminate in the Second Coming of Christ. The spirituals complemented Olivi's reflections by specifying that Pope John was the antichrist that the Apocalypse expected to appear in this era and took the fact that the majority of the Church sympathized with their brother Franciscans, the so-called "conventuals" as an indication that most of the Church had lapsed into heresy, in what was one of the great cataclysms predicted by the Apocalypse before the end. Finally, the spirituals agreed with their brother Peter John that the right understanding of Francis' teaching on poverty was crucial and contended that Popes Gregory and Nicholas had interpreted that teaching correctly.

John XXII was not impressed with their arguments. In 1323 he condemned their doctrine, suppressed their houses, and exiled their leaders, Michael of Cesna and William of Ockham. On May 24, 1324, Ockham and a number of his supporters with the connivance of Louis of Bavaria issued the Sachsenhausen Appeal, a refutation of John and an appeal for a general council to declare John a heretic. Their appeal fell on deaf ears.[16]

A fitting epitaph for the attempts of the conciliarists and infallibilists to restrict papal discretion in the Middle Ages can be gleaned from the decree for the Greeks issued at the Council of Florence (1438–45):

> We decree that the Holy Apostolic See and the Roman Pontiff have primacy
> in the whole world, and that this Roman Pontiff is the successor of blessed

---

[16] Brian Tierney, *Origins of Papal Infallibility* (Leiden: E. J. Brill, 1972).

Peter, Prince of the Apostles, and true vicar of Christ, head of the whole church and father and teacher of all Christians; that to him in Blessed Peter was given by our Lord Jesus Christ the full power of feeding, ruling and governing the universal church as it is contained in the acts of the ecumenical councils and in the sacred canons.

From Martin V onward popes regained the initiative in the Church and, after summoning a few general councils, succeeded in turning *Frequens* into a dead letter. As the medieval period drew to a close Christians remained convinced that the Church needed reform in both its head and its members, but they saw few signs of hope for such a reform, especially if it had to occur under the direction of the pope in Rome.[17]

Reformation and Trent

"At the beginning of the sixteenth century everyone that mattered in the Western Church was crying out for Reformation."[18] Chadwick's assessment describes well the state of the Church at the outset of the modern period. What reformation advocates wanted, however, was not doctrinal reform alone, but administrative, legal, and moral reform, especially of the clergy. Its inadequate training and general ignorance, the absorption of the papacy in politics, and bureaucratic centralization, particularly in the processes of ecclesiastical litigation and appeal, led high-minded Catholics almost to despair of the situation. Finally, the failures of Constance, Basel, and Lateran V (1512–17), made people extremely cynical about the prospects for reformation in the Church, especially if Rome had to lead the way.

Erasmus is reported to have said that any layman would be insulted were he to be called a priest, a cleric, or a monk. A sixteenth-century proverb reads, "Better to meet a robber than a begging friar." Thomas More described well the state of theology at the time when he said that he might as soon obtain bodily nourishment by milking a he-goat into a sieve as spiritual nourishment by reading the schoolmen.

Simony had once again become widespread in the Church. The papacy in particular had become highly desirable because its incumbent had two thousand marketable jobs at his disposal. Albrecht of Brandenburg paid ten thousand ducats for the bishopric of Mainz. After the inflation that had ravaged Europe in the fifteenth century, he required two more

---

[17] Besides the works already cited, one other source was also helpful in compiling this section: Anton Weiler, "Church Authority and Government in the Middle Ages," *Historical Problems of Church Renewal*, Concilium 7 (Glenrock, N.J.: Paulist, 1965) 123–36.

[18] Owen Chadwick, *The Reformation* (Middlesex: Penguin, 1964) 11.

episcopal sees and numerous abbeys to support him in the fashion he judged his due. It was Albrecht who obtained from the pope the indulgences he needed to send preachers around Germany as his fundraisers to pay off his simoniac debts. Simony was so prevalent that, when Martin Luther nailed his theses to the door, only 7 percent of German pastors were actually resident in their parishes. Antoine du Prat, archbishop of Sens in France, entered his cathedral for the first time at his funeral. In some cities of southern Germany, 10 percent of the male population was ordained to say Mass for the repose of the dead who had left a particular church benefactions for that purpose.

Furthermore, many ecclesiastical offices had again come under the control of civil officials. Linacre, physician to Henry VIII, was rector of four parishes and canon in three cathedrals. From 1450 to 1520 Geneva had five ducal bishops, two of whom were eight years old at the time of their nominations.

While secular rulers gained strength in the Church and in their realms, the papacy Luther confronted was a papacy considerably weakened by comparison with the breadth of Innocent III's power. In Spain the power of Ferdinand and Isabella considerably outstripped that of their predecessors. The same could be said for Henry VII and his son Henry VIII in England and the princes in Germany as a group. Only in France and Poland did the nobility exercise some kind of a check on princely power. These stronger monarchs were able to seize powers heretofore considered rights of local churches. In 1478 Sixtus IV conceded to Spanish sovereigns control of the inquisition in that country. In 1516 the pope signed a concordat at Bologna with the French king acceding to him the appointment of all higher clergy for France (82 bishops, 10 archbishops, and 527 abbots) and narrowing the rights of appeal to Rome for the French clergy.

Finally there was the new learning. The merchant class was becoming better educated. The printing press made possible a freer and wider diffusion of ideas. From the twelfth century onward a hue and cry of protest had been raised against the ecclesiastical system in the name of the Christian ideal of life based on a return to the Scriptures. In the sixteenth century Erasmus was a typical representative of this tradition of protests. His *Praise of Folly* (1511) and *The Colloquies* (1518) raised the consciousness of the educated public about abuses in the Church. In these texts he ridiculed ecclesiastical corruption and graft, popular superstition, and idolatrous practices. He lowered the already low reputation of popes and clergy, monks and friars, and most especially theologians.

The details of the Protestant Reformation need not detain us here, but we should note two disastrous consequences it had for the Roman Catholic

Church: for one, it took out from the Church the majority of those people who saw Rome as a major stumbling block and the local congregation as the best place to begin reform. It also (at least in its Anabaptist phase) removed most of the charismatic (or liminal) elements. As a result the very genuine reform that the Council of Trent (1545–63) achieved was centered on Rome and the Church as an institution.

Trent in fact had little to say in the area of ecclesiology. Most of the conciliarist bishops had remained aligned to Rome, and the council began with a great fear that there would be a renewed attempt to limit papal primacy and reinstate the requirement of a general council at regular intervals.

On April 8, 1546, the council published one of its first documents, *De Canonicis Scripturis* (On the Canonical Scriptures). In it the fathers of the council bypassed the question whether there were one or two sources (Scripture and Tradition) for the faith of the Church. Their concern focused on conserving the essential elements of the gospel in their purity as a source of saving truth and moral discipline. For them there existed one font, the gospel found in written books and unwritten traditions.

The books include both Old and the New Testaments; and God is their author. The traditions "come from the mouth of Christ himself or are inspired by the Holy Spirit and have been preserved in continuous succession in the Catholic Church" (DS 1501).

The practical reforms of Trent were extensive. It centralized the control of the Inquisition in Rome. It set up the first Index of Books for the universal Church, reformed the liturgy by establishing a Roman Missal and breviary for the whole Church, and allowed Pius IV to publish a catechism in its name which became *the* model for instruction in the Catholic faith. Trent also introduced an interesting novelty: a Congregation of the Council. Medieval councils had simply published their decrees and left their interpretation to competent theologians and canonists. After Trent all disputes about the meaning of particular passages needed to be submitted to the Congregation for assessment.[19]

Yves Congar has argued that the Tridentine reform had two especially important effects. First of all, it reasserted a centralized Church authority to a degree unknown in the Middle Ages. The rights of medieval sovereigns, including popes and bishops, had always been tempered by the rights of the corporation. After Trent the subject of law in the Church was the individual endowed with authority, and the ideal authority figure was a

---

[19] Michael Place, "From Solicitude to Magisterium: Theologians and Magisterium from the Council of Trent to the First Vatican Council," *Chicago Studies* 17 (1978) 228–29.

supreme, personal sovereign bishop or pope to whom the local or universal Church was subjected. Through Trent the individual Catholic came progressively into more immediate contact with the pope. First Roman catechisms, then papal encyclicals (an eighteenth-century development) told Catholics what Rome thought on the Catholic faith and related topics. The Roman Missal regulated their worship. Roman documents also stipulated fasting customs, canonical preparation for marriage, and the seminary education of future priests. Religious institutes now needed Roman authorization before they could operate freely even in a local church. After Trent, Roman interventions in local churches increased and a sharp Roman eye was kept on any religious publication, especially theological books and catechisms. All these practices, now taken for granted by Roman Catholics, were innovations of the Tridentine reform.

Secondly, Congar observes, after Trent authoritative teaching came to dominate moral and pastoral ideas and practices. The authority of God came to be seen as physically and automatically present in ecclesiastically institutionalized forms of authority. Little gap existed between the divine authority as an absolute standard and its instantiation in moral and pastoral pronouncements by Church officials. Catholics heard God's voice in these pronouncements, and the room for appraisal progressively diminished.[20]

At the end of the sixteenth century Robert Bellarmine stated: "The one and true church is the community of men brought together by the profession of the same Christian faith, and conjoined in the communion of the same sacraments, under the government of legitimate pastors and especially the one Vicar of Christ on earth, the Roman pontiff."[21] This definition of the Church is significant because it became the one regularly cited in the manuals of ecclesiology Roman Catholic seminarians studied. Bellarmine undoubtedly understood his definition in the fullest sense. Profession of the same faith, communion in the same sacraments, and government of legitimate pastors were all for him essentials of the true Church. Because Anglicans and especially the Orthodox arguably shared in these essentials, "under the Roman Pontiff" became *the* essential of Roman Catholicism. Even in its best interpretation, however, the definition has its shortcomings. The first essential excludes from the people of God pagans, Muslims, Jews, heretics, and apostates; the second, catechumens and the excommunicated; the third, schismatics. For Bellarmine, the Church was

---

[20] Congar, "The Historical Development of Authority in the Church," 144–45, and Place, "From Solicitude to Magisterium," 228.

[21] As cited by Avery Dulles in *Models of the Church* (Garden City, N.Y.: Doubleday, 1974) 14; the original Latin text can be found in Bellarmine's *De Controversiis,* Tome 2, Liber 3 (Naples: Giuliano, 1857) 2:75.

understood as a visible society, "as visible and palpable as the community of the Roman people, or the Kingdom of France, or the Republic of Venice."[22] In his writings, ecclesiology becomes hierarchology, the Church a fixed and set structure of offices where issues of authority are paramount. Bellarmine also saw the Church as composed of interior elements of faith, hope, charity, and grace, and so forth, which were related to the visible society as soul to the body. It is noteworthy, however, that subsequent generations remembered as his "definition" only what he said of the visible body.

Ecclesiology Against Modernity

At the inception of the nineteenth century, papal infallibility would have been questioned by the majority of Roman Catholics except those in Italy, some parts of Spain, and a few eccentrics in France.[23] Part of the reason for this was that the French and German churches had a long tradition of independence from Rome. Napoleon changed all that. When he came to power, there were over fifty French bishops in exile from the revolution. Since many of them were royalists, Napoleon proposed a reorganization of the French church so that its dioceses corresponded to the sixty departments into which he had broken down the nation. Because the new dioceses did not correspond to the old, he suggested that new bishops be appointed. Since the exiled bishops were also by and large Gallicans (staunch defenders of the independence of the French hierarchy), Pius VII was only too happy to comply and appoint bishops more loyal to Rome. In conquered Germany, Napoleon reorganized the country in such a way that numerous bishops found themselves in new territories ruled by Protestant princes. As a result recourse to Rome became the standard means of protecting traditional privileges of local German churches. The means of transmitting doctrine in these nations changed as well. Before the revolution French clerics learned theology by direct study of conciliar and patristic sources under the tutelage of professors whose authority was enormous; after Napoleon they learned it from manuals that emphasized the authority of the pope and the local bishop. Before 1789 there were eighteen Catholic universities in Germany. In 1815 there remained five faculties of Catholic theology attached to state universities.[24]

---

[22] Dulles, *Models of the Church,* 14.

[23] Yves Congar, "L'écclesiologie, de la Revolution Française au Concile du Vatican, sous le signe de l'affirmation de l'autorité," *L'Ecclésiologie au Xixe Siècle* (Paris: Unam Sanctam, 1960) 97.

[24] Ibid., 90–99.

In the nineteenth century the secular world proved extremely hostile to the Catholic Church. Rationalism dominated the intellectual scene and sneered at people who acted on faith or authority. Many secularists believed religion would vanish with the progress of time, and hierarchical structures were consigned to oblivion. Liberalism pressed the case of the budding democracies not only against the monarchs but also against any churches, like the Catholic, that supported the royalty and had monarchical government. The free individual assumed center stage. Autonomy of conscience was his badge. Religion, if it were to be tolerated, could be only a private affair. It was the state, and not the Church, that had responsibility for harmony in the public sphere. In this atmosphere, a number of very powerful states emerged which, in the course of time and by use of concordats, were able to bring the election of bishops under civil control. In some cases these concordats enshrined long-standing customs; in others they gave the appointment of bishops over to secular rulers. Eventually the pope could directly appoint bishops only in the papal states, Greece, Albania, and mission countries.

Not all Catholics were happy with this turn of events and they generally turned to Rome in their discontent. Apologetic tracts emphasized the impotence of reason and the need for divine teaching. Sermons spoke of the Church as a mother to whom obedience was owed and a source of stability in the midst of the chaos of questioning and uncertainty. To believe in the Church was to accept what its priests, its bishops, its pope taught. With time an immense devotion to the reigning pope grew among nineteenth-century Catholics. He was seen as an underdog pawn in politics, a clear and lasting beacon in the turmoil of the times.[25] If the Church was losing its political power (and the pope would be deprived of the Papal States forty years later), the battle for the minds of Catholics was just beginning.

In 1824 Leo XII had restored the Roman College (predecessor of today's Gregorian University) to the Jesuits. Its first luminous figure was Giovanni Perrone. He taught that the Church was the Mystical Body, meaning that the Church was the visible continuation of Christ's incarnation, a union of divine and human elements in one moral person. The Church was the bodily expression of Christ on earth who was her vivifying principle. Christ had endowed the Church with a teaching office which as witness proposed truths of faith, as judge settled controversies of faith, and as teacher daily instructed the faithful on faith and morals.

A later luminary of the Roman school, John Baptist Franzelin wrote that Christ, having established himself as divine, commanded absolute obedience and faith as the appropriate response to his teaching. He conferred

---

[25] Place, "From Solicitude to Magisterium," 236.

this same teaching power on his disciples and continues to do so in regard to their successors as a whole under the headship of Peter who alone is a teacher of the universal Church. Christ bestowed on his Church a deposit of faith to be preserved and taught by a living, authentic magisterium until the end of time. Franzelin substituted the traditional Protestant description of Church power as teaching, sanctifying, and ruling for the Catholic distinction between orders and jurisdiction.

Domenico Palmieri and Camillo Mazzella, also faculty at the Roman College, insisted that ecclesial power is bestowed directly and immediately on the pope and (derivatively through him) on the bishops. The living magisterium teaches in Christ's name and can oblige the faithful to believe what it teaches. Bishops collectively dispersed throughout the world or together at a council cannot teach Catholic faith without papal concurrence, but the pope is infallible without consultation. Louis Billot taught that the orthodox sense of a dogma is the same as what the present magisterium teaches, and that this teaching is not different from the past. Finally, Timothy Zapelena pointed out that the Church must be infallible because God could not justifiably oblige the faithful to assent under pain of loss of eternal life if the Church could err when it proposes a doctrine as to be believed under pain of such loss.

A number of assumptions bound together all the Jesuits who taught at the Roman College from 1824 to 1870. The Church was a visible, supernatural society which shared in some aspects of its founder's divinity. Its government was a monarchy where God gives supreme power to a ruler directly and a pyramid whose unity depends on subordination of people to bishops, of bishops to the pope, of the pope to Christ, and Christ to the Father. There are two types of members in the Church: superiors and subjects. Authority in the Church provides stability and order. God wills that all be saved by accepting a truth revealed to some. This truth was given at the beginning, complete, unified, consistent, absolute, and immutable. Only its subjective appropriation occurs in time. It must be possible to know this truth which effects our eternal salvation with certainty. Doubt has no place in Catholic belief. All the data theology uses comes from the past; personal or communal experience in the present plays little or no role. Theology consists in conceptual clarification and refinement. In the theology of the Roman College there was little room for genuine doctrinal development, historical criticism, or uncertainty and open-endedness. In a few instances the Roman College theologians did concede that dissent might make a positive contribution.

In most nineteenth-century theology it was assumed that unity of the Church would only be explained on the basis of Church authority, and that to be one the Church required a visible principle of that unity. Thus the papacy became a divinely created office to preserve ecclesial unity. Christ was relegated to the role of founding the Church, and the Holy Spirit to the role of guaranteeing the infallible judgments of official teachers. The papal magisterium became an absolute spiritual sovereignty to be accorded unquestioning loyalty. Theological faculties were repeatedly reminded that the papal understanding of the faith was normative for the Church.[26]

There were dissenting voices. John Henry Newman and the Tübingen school come to mind. The latter's leading figure, Johann Adam Mohler, taught that it was the Holy Spirit who united the Church, first of all by uniting all Christians with one another, and also by joining the Church of today with its predecessors.[27] Mohler, however, did agree with Perrone that the Church visibly continued the incarnation. But dissenting voices in the nineteenth century were few and were drowned out by the steady drone of the papalist theologians.

Papal Infallibility

When the bishops of the Church responded to the call of Pius IX to come to the First Vatican Council, they were divided over the advisability of promulgating papal infallibility. The council, before it was adjourned two months before by the Italian army's invasion of Rome, did publish two decrees, one on the faith of the Church and the other on the Petrine primacy of the pope. This latter decree concludes with the solemn declaration about those instances when the pope enjoys the infallibility of the Church.

The decree on Petrine primacy forms the context of the definition. The introduction notes that, as the Father sent Christ, so he chose and sent apostles. That his faithful might be secure in one faith and communion, Christ set Peter over the rest of the apostles as the abiding principle and foundation of the unity of the Church. Chapter I, citing John 1:42, Matthew 16:16-19, and John 21:15-19, teaches that Peter was the prince of the apostles and head of the Church militant, having received from Christ himself a primacy of jurisdiction, not just of honor. The second chapter, on the basis of Irenaeus, the Council of Ephesus, and Leo the Great, teaches that Petrine primacy continues in the Roman pontiffs as Peter's successors by the institution of Christ. Chapter III asserts that the Roman pontiff has

[26] T. Howland Sanks, *Authority in the Church: A Study in Changing Paradigms* (Missoula, Mont.: American Academy of Religion, 1974). The theologians at the Roman College were typical for their times; it was not their originality, but their location that made their theology so important.

[27] Congar, *Tradition and Traditions,* 194.

ordinary (not just in his solemn acts) and immediate jurisdiction over all churches, all pastors, and all the faithful. He has the right of free communication to all pastors and faithful regarding faith and morals, discipline and government. They must submit to his power. He is supreme judge in the Church; all may have recourse to his tribunal; no one may reopen a judgment of the Apostolic See. He has the fullness of power in the Church which does not prejudice episcopal power but strengthens and protects it. In Chapter IV the council fathers, alluding to Constantinople IV, Lyons II, and Florence that Rome had kept the faith undefiled and enjoyed supreme and full primacy over the whole Catholic Church, speak of the infallible magisterium of the Roman pontiff. It is a gift of the Holy Spirit not to make new doctrine, but to preserve the deposit of faith inviolable and faithfully. The gift was made to Peter and his successors that they might teach the truth and a never-failing faith for the salvation of all. The content of these chapters is not part of the solemn definition of papal infallibility. It is, therefore, subject to revision within limits regarding both its wording and its content.

The solemn definition reads as follows:

> Therefore, faithfully adhering to the tradition received from the beginning of the Christian faith, for the glory of God our Saviour, the exaltation of the Catholic religion and the salvation of Christian peoples, the Sacred Council approving, we teach and define that it is a dogma divinely revealed: that the Roman Pontiff, when he speaks *ex cathedra,* that is, when in discharge of the office of Pastor and Doctor of all Christians, by virtue of his supreme apostolic authority he defines a doctrine regarding faith or morals to be held by the Universal Church, by the divine assistance promised him in Blessed Peter, is possessed of the infallibility with which the Divine Redeemer willed that his church should be endowed for defining the doctrine regarding faith or morals: and that therefore such definitions of the Roman Pontiff are irreformable of themselves, and not from the consent of the Church. But if any one—which God avert—presume to contradict this our definition—anathema sit.

With this definition the council sets a number of conditions which must be met for papal infallibility to occur: first, the pope must speak *ex cathedra,* that is, in his official capacity as pope and not as an individual; secondly, he invokes his supreme apostolic authority; third, the doctrine defined concerns faith or morals; finally, he is teaching all Christians and intends to bind the universal Church regarding its faith. Roman Catholic theologians usually teach that there have been only two occasions when these four conditions have been met: the promulgation of the dogma of the Immaculate Conception of Mary by Pius IX in 1854 and of her Assumption by

Pius XII in 1950. Faith and morals in the mind of the council seem to be two separate realms, faith a conceptual formulation in dogmas and morals in ethical propositions. The two aforesaid dogmas would be examples of faith. The phrase "Faith and Morals" goes back to a letter of Augustine to a priest named Januarius, and the issue in that letter seems to be local liturgical customs. Up to and including the Council of Trent, the phrase *fides et mores* operated as a unit, although the medievals did distinguish between faith (Church doctrine, liturgical-sacramental practice, and canonical traditions) and customs which included the various sacramental traditions. Faith and customs was a term comprehending the whole faith life of the Church. Thus, the First Vatican Council's use of *fides et mores* is clearly an example of doctrinal development.

The infallibility in question is not a personal prerogative of the pope even in his official capacities, but a gift of Christ to the Church for defining faith and morals. In a sense the Roman Catholic Church has no doctrine of papal infallibility; it has a doctrine that specifies when the pope participates in the infallibility of the Church. The minutes of the council specify that this infallibility is to be distinguished from the absolute infallibility of God. Although we can reasonably assume that most of the fathers at the council had in mind a definition of infallibility as immunity from error, the council itself did not consecrate that definition as an official interpretation.

The most misunderstood and misconstrued phrase in the definition is "such definitions of the Roman Pontiff are irreformable of themselves, and not from the consent of the church." The minutes of the council make clear that the phrase "not from the consent of the church" is directed at the Gallican contention that papal pronouncements can only be infallible after the national churches have ratified them and that "irreformable of themselves" means that the definitions are true because they agree with the deposit of faith. Many Roman Catholic theologians today contend that, since the council repudiated an attempt to include a solemn formula whereby the Church would know automatically that the pope was solemnly defining, reception of definitions by the Church is not precluded by Vatican I as necessary for a determination whether the pope has spoken infallibly. The council's definition does not necessarily leave to the Roman pontiff the decision whether his teaching is infallible. It remains for the Church dispersed throughout the world to receive what is said as consonant with the deposit of faith. Canon law notes that "no doctrine is understood as infallibly defined unless this fact is manifestly established" (Can. 749, no. 3). My own opinion, further, is that Vatican I's definition is compatible with the medieval thesis that a pope can be a heretic. The Church in its process of reception would distinguish whether what the pope uttered in an apparently solemn fashion was in fact heresy or a definition of faith.

Finally, Vatican I did not teach that the primacy of Peter now resident in the Bishop of Rome can only reside in Rome. The Avignon papacy disproves that. Nor does its teaching require that the primacy can only be exercised by an individual. One could argue that in the years 1414–15, the Council of Constance exercised that primacy in deposing three claimants to the papacy and electing a fourth. This is not to say that the Petrine primacy should not reside in the Bishop of Rome.[28]

Vatican Council II

While almost a hundred years later Vatican II reaffirmed the primacy of the Roman pontiff in strong terms, it also situated the primacy in the context of the college of bishops and treated authority in the Church as something that can reach beyond the episcopal order. Vatican II emphasized that it is bishops who are possessed of the fullness of the priesthood to teach and govern as its shepherds: that is, it is the local bishop, and not the parish priest, who should constitute our paradigm of what a priest is. That bishop belongs to a college which, in succession to the apostles and by appointment of the Holy Spirit, links all bishops to one another and has concern and responsibility for the whole Church. It is this college in union with and under its head, the pope, which has supreme power over the universal Church. In their local churches, bishops enjoy proper, ordinary, and immediate power by virtue of their consecration which is exercised in Christ's name, but can be regulated and circumscribed within limits by the pope. As vicars of Christ, they counsel, exhort, and, by example, edify their flocks to grow in truth and holiness. They have the right and duty to make laws, to pass judgment on subjects, and to moderate both the liturgies and apostolates of their particular churches. These liturgies are Church celebrations and sacraments of unity for local churches under their bishops. Together with the other bishops of the region (normally a nation), they are charged with working out the necessary local liturgical adaptations and marriage rites. They are entitled to full and perfect freedom and independence from civil authorities whenever they speak with the Apos-

---

[28] Edward Cuthbert Butler, *The Vatican Council 1867–70,* ed. Christopher Butler (Westminster, Md.: Newman, 1962); Maurice Duchaine, "Vatican I on Primacy and Infallibility," *Papal Primacy and the Universal Church,* 139–50; Avery Dulles, "Papal Authority in Roman Catholicism," *A Pope for All Christians,* ed. Peter McCord (N.Y.: Paulist, 1976) 48–70; Derek Holmes, *The Triumph of the Holy See* (London: Burns and Oates, 1978).

tolic See, their subjects, or other ecclesiastical authorities. In all these actions they are to conduct themselves as servants.

Eastern-Rite patriarchs along with their synods constitute the superior authority for all affairs within the patriarchate. This authority enables them to establish new eparchies and nominate bishops, to determine the languages to be used in liturgies, and to approve translations into the vernacular of liturgical texts after they have reported their action to the Holy See. The Roman pontiff has the right to intervene in individual cases.

The college of bishops has no authority unless it is conceived of in union with its head, the Roman pontiff, who, as Vicar of Christ and pastor of the whole Church, is endowed with full, supreme, universal power over the Church which can always be exercised freely. A council is only ecumenical if confirmed or accepted by the successor of Peter. It is a papal prerogative to convoke, preside over, and confirm such councils. The Roman pontiff can call bishops living in all parts of the world to collegial action and accept or approve the unified teaching and action of bishops dispersed throughout the world. In virtue of his primacy, the pope can remove any institute of perfection (a religious community) or individual members thereof from the jurisdiction of local ordinaries. In the Roman Rite, the right to nominate and appoint bishops belongs to the pope.

According to Vatican II, much apostolic work in the Church is begun by initiative of the laity, and, although this work needs to be regulated by prudent judgment, lay people should not be deprived of acting of their own accord. But only works which have received official approval can claim the name "Catholic." Since sincere people may legitimately disagree on certain matters, no one may appropriate "Catholic" for his or her opinion.

Several models of Church operate in the documents of Vatican II. One is institutional and leads the council to speak again and again of ecclesiastical jurisdiction and the centrality of hierarchy in Roman Catholic thinking. A second is the Mystical Body of Christ. According to a third model the Church is a sacrament of the gracious triune God, and its jurisdiction and hierarchical order exist for the spiritual gifts of the Church which reach their apogee in the celebration of the Eucharist by a local congregation. Finally, the Church is the pilgrim People of God. As a visible society, it needs structures and offices which are, the council repeatedly stresses, to be exercised as services. The Church is on the way, has not achieved its goal, and is ever in need of purification and reform. Thus, the Church is neither identified with nor does it share in the glory and triumph of its founder, Jesus Christ. The council highlights the communal responsibility of the episcopal college in union with its head and the covenant of the whole people with the God of Jesus Christ. While there are frequent echoes of the individualism and juridicism of a document that Vatican Council I never promulgated [*De ecclesia* (On the Church)], both aspects are relativized in the documents of Vatican II.[29]

[29] Yves Congar, *L'église* (Paris: Editions de Cerf, 1970); Charles Moeller, "History of *Lumen Gentium's* Structure and Ideas," *Vatican II: An Interfaith Appraisal,* ed. John Miller (Notre Dame, Ind.: University of Notre Dame Press, 1961) 123–52; *Commentary on the Documents of Vatican II* (N.Y.: Herder and Herder, 1967) 1:105–305.

CHAPTER 6

The Conclusion

History and Theory

The first question that requires asking is whether the survey of the history of authority in the Church in chapters four and five confirms the general theory laid down in chapter three. At first it would seem that a formidable objection arises from the very beginnings of the Church's history: the reluctance of the New Testament to use the word *exousia* in regard to the Church. This word translated from Greek as "authority" is admittedly regarded with suspicion because of an understanding of authority in the secular sphere as necessarily implying "lording it over" other people. Yet the New Testament also does not hesitate to present Jesus as someone who speaks and acts with authority, a speaking and acting which characterizes the ministry of his disciples after his resurrection gift to them of the Holy Spirit. That ministry is to be carried out as a service of God and the community. It is thus not authority as such that the New Testament writers contest, but the attitude of "lording it over."

The first thesis of chapter three stated the importance of authority for the community: authority functions for a community in a manner analogous to the function of freedom in the life of a human individual. In the New Testament the authority of Jesus is central. Following him on the way of his public ministry constitutes the demand laid on anyone claiming to be his disciple. As the risen one he communicates the authority he has received from the Father to all of his disciples. The primitive Church did not state the importance of Jesus' authority baldly, but it simply took for granted that his authoritative actions and words are what the community is all about.

In the second century the evolution of Church government from two forms, the presbyterate and monoepiscopacy in different places to the monarchical bishop everywhere, was tied to what the early Church conceived as its principal mark: the unity of the members as representative of the oneness of God. Ignatius of Antioch saw this unity as a harmony of many instruments producing a single piece of music. At this point the unity in question was primarily that of the local church. In later centuries the Church sought to express the same unity more universally in synods and councils. During the Middle Ages the notion of the Church as a corporation raised the significance of a proper understanding of authority for the very being of the Church. More recently the nineteenth and twentieth centuries have made authority progressively a principal preoccupation for the Church's self-understanding.

One thing the New Testament makes very clear is that authority is to be self-effacing (service) and to be understood as vicarious (stewardship). Christian authority is always under God, through Jesus Christ, and in the Holy Spirit. The Middle Ages emphasize that God's authority alone is absolute. Vatican I obliquely acknowledged the same when it referred to absolute infallibility.

A second thesis of chapter three argued that authority was a human practice whereby one party was enabled to act or speak in the name of someone and at least one other assumed an obligation to speak and act accordingly; in this latter regard one can speak of obedience. In the New Testament Jesus has authority because he is empowered by God and lives his life in obedience to his Father. Disciples follow him by responding obediently to his call and are empowered to proclaim the Good News by the Holy Spirit. Paul likewise claims to be so empowered and grounds that claim in his obedient following of Jesus. He acknowledges that others have charisms from the Spirit and summons them to obey the demands of the gospel. This dialectic of an empowerment, principally to proclaim the Good News boldly, and an obligation laid on hearers of that word constitutes the New Testament practice of Christian authority.

In subsequent ages Clement wrote to Corinth in the name of the Roman community; bishops were understood to speak for their local churches; groups of bishops spoke for the church of a region and, from 325 onward, for the Church universal. A consistent claim of the bishops of Rome was that they spoke in the name of Peter and eventually as Vicars of Christ. The history of the Church makes abundantly clear that when members of the Church felt that these claims were legitimate, they almost always acknowledged an obligation to respond in obedience.

Thirdly, chapter three asserted that authority takes two forms: *an* authority and *in* authority. *An* authority is authoritative because it displays the virtues the community holds in esteem. *In* authority is grounded in custom, regulations, or law. There can be no question that initially in the Church most authority was conceived of as *an* authority. In fact we could well depict the New Testament as an exercise in laying down the virtues required for being a Christian as exemplified in the figure of Jesus. Paul constitutes the paradigmatic figure of one who claimed authority because he displayed in his words and actions the virtues of following Jesus. Paul, however, did claim that he was called by God in the risen Christ to be an apostle; similarly, in the Gospels, the disciples were commissioned by Jesus to proclaim the Good News officially in sayings such as "the one who hears you, hears me." Only in the Pastoral epistles does the issue of *in* authority come prominently into play, and even there the author emphasizes the virtues needed to be a good presbyter. The New Testament regularly sees authority as a matter of the charisms which are given in the Spirit for the building up of the whole community.

By the beginning of the second century the need for structure and *in* authority became evident. The *Didache* argued that Church government was necessary. Initially communities divided over the form of *in* authority, and eventually monoepiscopacy prevailed. A century later bishops began to be seen as mediators between God and their communities. Both Cyprian and the *Didascalia* saw the bishop as someone set over the community. In the early Church, however, the concept of *an* authority did not vanish. The authority of martyrs, holy people, and monks remained great, and bishops were regularly expected to exemplify the virtues these *an* authorities displayed.

In the Middle Ages papal authority over the whole Church came to the fore in the West. In fact the medievals saw the authority of God as specially communicated to the *majores,* whether they be bishops and abbots as teachers of the faith or masters of theology in the universities. Nonetheless, conciliarism sought to keep alive in the Church the notion of a widespread distribution of authority in the Church which remained the rule in the East. During the Avignon Schism canonists insisted that the unity of the Church had been preserved by the sacramental and moral life of the faithful. Religious communities emerged so that *an* authority might find a home.

Since the Reformation there can be little doubt that Roman Catholic ecclesiology has been preoccupied with juridical, that is, structural views of authority, and has, as a consequence, viewed authority in the Church almost exclusively as *in* authority. But the authority of a virtuous life never did cease to lay claim to certain Catholic allegiances, and the welcome accorded to Vatican II was no doubt in part because the council restored balance in the Church's understanding of authority.

Fourth, authority is grounded in the authoritative or the tradition as both inherited from the past and evolving into the future. The importance of tradition for the Church leaps off the pages of its history. The Gospels themselves are an example of tradition as here depicted: they both preserve the words and deeds of Jesus and apply them to new situations in the Church. At the same time they do not hesitate to judge claims for authority in the primitive Church on the basis of the foundational beliefs and values of the community.

Throughout the period of the early Church the faithful handing on of the apostolic tradition proved crucial. The early Church required that all proposed innovations (*homoousion,* for instance) be shown to be consistent with the Scriptures as interpreted especially in the churches of apostolic origin. People were judged orthodox or heretical according to the understanding of that tradition of interpretation.

Rome based its claim to authority in the West on the fact that it alone among all local churches possessed an apostolic tradition. On this ground it reserved to itself judgments on what innovations could be accepted. Popes themselves were evaluated in the Church in terms of the fidelity of their pronouncements to the great ecumenical councils and what their predecessors had said.

Finally, dissent is required for the appropriate exercise of authority in the Church. The patron saint of dissent in the Church is the apostle Paul who differed from Peter, James, and the mother church of Jerusalem on the necessity of Jewish practices for Gentile converts. In the years 359 and 360 dissenting believers kept the faith of Nicea alive in the Church. Leo I and Leo II did not hesitate to dissent from ecumenical councils and approve only some of the conciliar decrees. In the ninth century Alcuin offered an example of moderate dissent from what he considered excessive papal claims. In the eleventh century the clergy of various European cities obviously thought it their right to take issue with the Gregorian reforms.

Even the declaration of papal infallibility came about because certain people early in the nineteenth century were willing to propose that doctrine in the face of a majority which questioned its wisdom. Much of what Vatican II taught involved embracing opinions of theologians who had been roundly condemned prior to the council. One thinks of John Courtney Murray and The Declaration on Religious Liberty.

The Distinctiveness of Christian Authority

A second question that the history of authority in the Church raises is: What are the distinctive features of Christian and Roman Catholic authority? The first characteristic that comes to mind is the mystical character of all Christian authority: it is under the God who liberated the people of Israel in the Exodus, remained faithful as their covenant partner in spite of their sinfulness, and has been revealed in the end times as the Father of our Lord Jesus Christ. He has shared fully his sovereign authority with the risen Christ who now communicates this authority to his graced but stumbling followers in the Holy Spirit. Thus, Christian authority is understood in the context of the story of God's unbounded love and mercy which calls every man and woman into the divine mystery as God's adopted sons and daughters. This call issues in a following of Jesus on the way where the cross is the paradigm of discipleship, and humility and a willingness to suffer are counted as blessings for the one who desires to be like Jesus. Any person in authority, then, wants to enhance the union of all men and women with this gracious God and with one another in the body of Christ. The unity the Church seeks is oneness in Christ Jesus under the inspiration of the Holy Spirit whose action is pluriform but conspires towards this oneness.

Secondly, all Christian authority needs to be understood eschatologically. The Church is the pilgrim People of God. It is only an inadequate sign of the union of all humanity with God and one another. While it never ceases to aspire towards and hope for that total unity, it tries to gather together and nurture those people who are already following Jesus on his way in a world torn apart by sin. It attempts to be a fellowship of loving service in the truth of Christ. As a consequence, Christian authority plays an ambiguous role. It strives to foster a Church which concretizes the hope of all men and women becoming one in Christ Jesus even though it knows all too well that it is often powerless to fend off the forces of destruction both around and within the Church. Thus authority in the Christian sense, that is, following Christ under the tutelage of the Spirit, is itself a pilgrimage. It is constantly in need of conversion and reformation even as it proceeds in the confidence that the gracious love that is the gift of the Holy Spirit has touched and continues to touch its exercise profoundly.

Finally, Christian authority is sacramental. From the beginning it has been a matter of proclaiming the Word boldly in the context of the Lord's Supper. It proceeds on the conviction that any Christian who can call God Abba has nothing to fear from a hostile world. Thus the Church makes bold to preach and teach and celebrate the Good News it proclaims—what God has done in Jesus Christ—in the Eucharist. Even a cursory examination of the Church's history reveals a preoccupation with teaching and doctrine that sets it apart from many other world religions. It is by reason of the given that authority in the Church is sacramental in the sense explained here that much Christian authority has naturally devolved upon those who are commissioned to preach the Word and preside at the Eucharist.

The mystical character of Christian authority relativizes its visible embodiment in any single person, group of persons, or even the whole body of the faithful. Its eschatological character requires that the propensity towards the sacerdotal just noted be seen as an inadequate (graced but nonetheless sinful) sign. The sacramental character becomes the norm by which hierarchical and juridical aspects of Church authority are judged. Offices and legal entitlements exist in the Church that local assemblies might gather to proclaim the Word and celebrate the Eucharist.

The Marks of Roman Catholic Authority

What constitute the distinctive features of Roman Catholic authority? First of all, baptism authorizes all members of the Church as pilgrims under God to proclaim the Word and celebrate the Eucharist, especially in their lives of service to God and one another. Secondly, ordination authorizes some members of the Church and enjoins on them special obligations, regarding that proclamation and celebration. The Church is endowed with an episcopal order which has a head who holds primacy. (One can hardly ignore the concern in Roman Catholic narrations of Church history with claims to Petrine primacy by the bishops of Rome.) Roman Catholic authority involves a dialectical interplay between its episcopate and the primate and between the episcopal order and the body faithful. While the dialectic is very real, the poles are not genuinely opposites. The primate is a bishop as well as being a head. The episcopate is composed of people who are baptized. And baptism remains for all the foundation for receiving the preeminent gift of the Holy Spirit.

Before we proceed to examine more closely the poles of the two dialectics we need to notice a profound change that has occurred in the Church's self-consciousness beginning with Vatican II. The pilgrim People of God is a world Church in the sense that it proclaims and celebrates the Good News for and in a world where those outside the Church set the agenda. As a consequence the primitive and the early churches before Constantine's edict of toleration are more helpful than the Constantinian, medieval, or modern churches for understanding how ecclesiastical authority should operate today and in the future. It is only natural that increasingly Church teaching has turned from preoccupation with inner-church problems to concern with peace, justice, and other issues which dominate the world scene. The Church tries to bring the riches of its tradition to bear upon situations beyond its control and hear the call of the Lord within those situations. It seeks to inculturate itself in what is different and sometimes alien.

The Episcopate in the Church

From the very beginning of its existence the Church has set some of its members apart as bishops or overseers. Early on these members were granted the exclusive privilege of presiding over the Eucharist and a pre-eminent role in the Church's preaching and teaching. They carried out these duties as representatives of the eschatological Lord. The fact that they, and not all, preached the Word and recited the Eucharistic Prayer at liturgical celebrations reminded the whole Church of its not-yet character. All are not one in Christ while the Church continues on her pilgrimage.[1]

A bishop upon his consecration enters the college of the bishops. As such, he assumes an obligation of solicitude for the universal Church. He and his brother bishops in union with the head of the college, the pope, bear responsibility for the bond of unity that is to characterize Christ's Church and possess full and supreme power over the universal Church. They are responsible for maintaining communion with God and among their geographically separated communities. They can express this over-arching unity either in ecumenical councils or dispersed throughout the world.

Bishops are also leaders of their local churches. As such they concretize the unity of all the members of a diocese with one another and foster the desire of that church for universal communion. Ordination is the one sacrament where, according to traditional Roman Catholic theology, grace is conferred not for the sake of the recipient but for the people to be served. Similarly bishops are consecrated for the service of their faithful. The faith they are to proclaim is simultaneously the faith of the Church universal as it has been handed down and preserved by the apostolic college and as it has been received in the local church.

The first duty of the bishops is to proclaim the Word. In large part they fulfill this duty in their role as teachers of the Church. They are principally responsible in the Church for the integrity of the doctrine taught and its consistency with the tradition. Their pastoral office alone can render binding judgments in the area of doctrine and issue authoritative formulations of the faith. While the hierarchy stands under and serves the Word of God, it alone authoritatively interprets that Word.

The Church requires a teaching authority because the human spirit can often misinterpret and misconstrue the meaning of the Scriptures. Thus the vulnerabilities of the human spirit call for a teaching authority which bears the special charge of fidelity to the tradition and harmony with living faith. Though the Holy Spirit touches the whole Church, it is a long tradition that the Spirit touches the pastors of the Church in a special way. Their teaching is entitled to the presumption of truth.

---

[1] Nicholas Lash in *Authority in a Changing Church* by John Dalrymple and others (London: Sheed and Ward, 1968).

To proclaim the Word in truth, bishops need to be hearers of the Word. Given the complexity of the issues about which they are called to teach, they need to take counsel of various experts—experts in the various branches of theology (exegesis, philosophical theology, ethics, canon law, pastoral theology) and the various sciences (natural, social, psychological), and also experts among the faithful living with the issues involved. Often the episcopal task will be managerial, seeing that the issues are probed at the necessary depth and with the requisite comprehensiveness. All hearers of the Word are engaged in a conversation both with the traditional wisdom of the Church and with the signs of the times. Mere repetition of what the Church has already said on some topic does not constitute fidelity to the tradition.

Church teaching is not indoctrination. It inspires as it instructs. It also leaves room for initiative on the part of those to whom it is directed.

There are two temptations a good bishop will resist. The first is the temptation to think that ordination or consecration have given him some special or unique access to the truth. In fact he has not been given a special charism of wisdom by the Holy Spirit, but a charge to evoke and facilitate the wisdom present in the entire community. While the talents he brings to his office may render him a colleague of some of the experts he needs to consult, he does not have a pipeline to what the Spirit wants to say. He speaks a word he heeds in the company of his fellow bishops and of the faithful.

The other temptation to be avoided is that of totalization. The bishop is not called to do everything for himself and for the People of God. The very call to holiness that his office enjoins must preclude this. He is called to be the least of the brothers and sisters. Thus, he should be the first to consult and be prepared to build consensus from below. His sensitivity to such counsel and reactions from the faithful will indicate how seriously he takes his role as teacher. In taking counsel and building consensus he approaches the episcopal ideal by his being able to recognize and acknowledge and even welcome an alien truth. Much of the bishop's effort, if he is to teach well, will go into his insuring that fairness and comprehensiveness are present in all his inquiries. Besides creating structures that insure these two qualities, he will see that crucial questions get asked and the tradition be clarified in light of present circumstances. It goes without saying that how the bishop carries out his consultation and builds consensus will differ whether he operates in a democratic society or under an authoritarian regime, in a country where Catholics form a majority or another where their status is that of a minority.[2]

---

[2] Rembert Weakland, "The Church in Worldly Affairs: Tensions Between Laity and Clergy," *America* (October 18, 1986) 201–05 and 215–16; Avery Dulles, "Authority, the Divided Legacy," *Commonweal* (July 12, 1985) 400–03.

Two kinds of assemblies of bishops since Vatican II have given special prominence to the episcopal teaching competence: national or regional bishops' conferences and the synod of bishops. National conferences of bishops have become an effective way of expressing the unity that bishops have with one another in the Holy Spirit. The bishops of a nation or region can collectively command resources that no single bishop in his own diocese could summon. Episcopal conferences have assumed increasing importance in the past twenty years for enhancing the teaching authority of all bishops. One only need think of the impact of Medellin and Puebla, the pastorals of the American bishops on nuclear arms and the world economy, or the letters of the Philippine bishops before and after the election that toppled Ferdinand Marcos. National conferences are not the college of bishops even for the territories over which the bishops in question collectively preside. But they have concretized for Roman Catholics around the world that their faith is a pluriform reality which is relevant to their everyday lives.

The process whereby the American bishops have developed their pastorals has provided an exemplary instance of how building consensus can be achieved in the Church. Their willingness to conduct hearings around the country in which numerous and conflicting viewpoints were heard, to work their thinking through several drafts which were open to criticism in the public forum, and yet to speak finally and forcefully unpleasant teachings to the nation they serve have provided a concrete example of how Church teaching might emerge from the totality of the Church under the tutelage of its bishops. Their tolerance of a counterpastoral on the economy by Roman Catholic laypersons has served to show their confidence that the word they proclaim has nothing to fear from a dissenting viewpoint. Such fearlessness is essential to episcopal authority especially because proclaiming the Word boldly today may mean proclaiming it in the face of hostile elements within the Church itself.[3]

The synod of bishops by contrast is a body which represents the entire episcopate. Eighty-five percent of its membership is elected by the various episcopal conferences, and it meets regularly to advise the pope about concerns of the universal Church. The pope convokes the synod and sets its agenda. The few documents synods have promulgated have been well received. The synods themselves do seem to have been deemed useful

[3] Ladislaus Orsy, "Episcopal Conferences, Their Theological Standing and Their Doctrinal Authority," *America* (November 8, 1980) 282–85; Avery Dulles, "Episcopal Conferences: Their Teaching Authority," *America* (January 13, 1990) 7–9; and Michael Novak, "The Authority of National Conferences of Bishops: Catholic Social Thought," *America* (January 13, 1990) 10–13, 21.

by the two popes who have called them. The synod form could perhaps be made more credible in the Church if the member bishops could also have some control over the synod's agenda.

The recently promulgated code of canon law has created a particular conundrum for local bishops in that it changes their responsibility in regard to the teaching of theology within their dioceses from exercising a negative vigilance (correcting errors as they arise and the erroneous if they are contumacious in their errors) to a positive deputation of all teachers of religion and theology. The canon in question seems to presume that teaching religious material is an extension of hierarchical teaching authority and not its own charism; thus it risks giving religion and theology teachers a different authority in the Church than what they should properly claim. In larger dioceses where there exist numerous Catholic schools the canon imposes an impossible burden on the bishops and runs the risk that any episcopal withholding or withdrawal of a canonical mission to teach will appear as necessarily arbitrary. Hopefully bishops will restrict their efforts to assuring that the procedures for appointing and evaluating such teachers are fair and responsible, and not extend them to the well-nigh impossible task of perusing each and every candidate for appointment or tenure. Otherwise not only is their oversight almost necessarily going to be arbitrary, but they risk placing serious obstacles to the freedom theological inquiry exacts while aggrandizing the authority of the presumably deputized teacher.[4]

Papal Primacy in the Church

The episcopal primacy of the pope is a firmly held belief of the Roman Catholic Church. In a very real sense the pope has full and supreme power over the universal Church. He alone can call his brother bishops to collegial action (in councils, for example), and he must participate in and approve of any of their collegial actions (whether in council or dispersed

---

[4] John Boyle, "Church Teaching Authority in the 1983 Code," *The Jurist* 45 (1985) 136–70. On Canon 812, see Sharon Euart, "Theologians and the Mandate to Teach," *Origins* 23 (1993) 465, 467–72; on the application of the canon to U.S. Catholic universities, see the following by bishops: James Malone, *Origins* 23 (1993) 472–74 and again *Origins* 23 (1994) 608–09, as well as John Leibrecht, *Origins* 23 (1994) 605, 607–08. For reactions from educators and theologians, see *Origins* 23 (1994) 610–14, and *Commonweal* 70 (November 19, 1993) 14–15, 22–26. The applications and reactions are developed in the context of the "Proposed Ordinances" of the U.S. Bishops for implementing *Ex corde ecclesiae* (cf. *Catholic Universities in Church and Society: A Dialogue on Ex Corde Ecclesiae,* ed. John Langan (Washington, D.C.: Georgetown University Press, 1993) 231–59.

throughout the world) if any such action is to have the force of law in the Church. His is a primacy of service to guard and promote the fidelity of all the local churches to Christ and to one another. Ideally the pope helps bishops as apostolic leaders in both their local churches and the Church universal. He encourages his fellow bishops to listen to and grow in love for one another. He urges them toward the fullness of Christian life and witness. He does not seek uniformity where legitimate diversity arises or to centralize administration of the church in Rome to the detriment of the authority of local churches.

The primatial ministry is best exercised not in isolation, but in collegial association. The primate needs both synodal and conciliar assistance plus regular consultation with his brother bishops if he is to overcome his personal, national, and theological limitations. The head and the college of bishops will attain the desired harmony that will make of papal primacy a credible sign if there exists a genuinely dialectical interplay of opinions to the mutual enrichment of both parties. The pope must both teach and hear the other bishops.

Papal authority exists in the service of and needs to be congruent with the truth, the gospel, the consciences and the faith of truly believing Christians. It is sometimes said that papal authority knows no juridical constraints. This is true if one examines the code of canon law. There exist, however, two moral constraints on papal exercise of jurisdiction by the very nature of the office, for popes are elected for the sake of the Church. Thereby they are constrained by (1) the Scriptures and the tradition of interpreting them in the Church, especially through the decrees of ecumenical councils, and (2) the faith of believers throughout the world. Popes are called to teach the faith of the Church in the sense of both these constraints and to make disciplinary decisions in light of this faith. They are not to teach their own personal opinions or those of a particular school of theology.

Vatican I decreed that the primacy of the pope is a primacy of jurisdiction. That is acceptable provided we understand the decree in a Vatican II sense that jurisdiction exists in the Church at the service of the sacramental. Papal primacy is first and foremost a liturgical leadership whereby the pope presides at Eucharists which call the whole Church together and in which he proclaims a salvific word. One of the significant contributions of the present papacy is that John Paul II, on his trips around the world, has restored an image in the minds of the faithful of the pope as someone who celebrates Eucharist and preaches to the People of God.

One current problem is that often Rome is perceived as not respecting the rights of local churches. Roman interventions seem to usurp the responsibilities of local bishops. Rome appears to be intent on imposing

Roman theology and custom everywhere in the Church and to equate communion with the head with abject submission to Roman demands. The claim that the pope possesses immediate jurisdiction over all Catholics becomes then a curse that breeds widespread scandal, especially when such jurisdiction strikes believing Catholics as an exercise that acknowledges no limits, not even moral ones, and insists on centralized power with little sensitivity to local needs and resources. The claim to immediate jurisdiction should be tempered by the principle of subsidiarity which has a long and illustrious standing in papal social encyclicals: the papacy should never try to do itself what can be done at the local level.

Church unity is not total uniformity in doctrinal expressions and practice. It is a unity in pluriformity. The primacy is called to foster and encourage the natural endowments and customs of local regions.

Sometimes certain Roman congregations or curial officials lose respect because they stand on their legal rights and give the impression that they have all the answers and are incapable of changing anything once it has been taught or done. Not only are all these characteristics of an insecure personality, but they belie the call of the Gospels for continued conversion. Such congregations might be better advised to share some doubts and questions along with their convictions and certainties and to make clear that the Roman word is not always the last word, but can be the first word in a continuing conversation. It is very interesting that Rome today gains in prestige whenever it admits a mistake or changes its mind.

Roman congregations can be of great service to the universal Church. They are situated in such a way that they can synthesize much of what is transpiring in the Church and make that wisdom available to all the local churches. When local differences, however, require filtering through a Roman lens in order to be validated, or Rome acts as if it is its prerogative to sit in judgment on local churches, the service that congregations in Rome might and often do offer gets lost from view. We might very well urge that Rome, in relation to the universal Church, perform the role it played in regard to the African church during the patristic period: the Roman prerogative then was to approve decisions made at the local or regional level and to return inadequate decisions to the lower levels for fuller consideration.

The Congregation for the Doctrine of the Faith was given the charge by Paul VI of encouraging the development of sound doctrine. When it does so, as it did in its second instruction on liberation theology, it truly contributes to the building up of the faith of the Church. But its negative judgments, especially on individual theologians, have left much to be desired. For instance, it is frequently not altogether clear that what it calls official teaching is not the theology of some person or of a particular school.

Additionally, the CDF has been resistant to what seem to be reasonable suggestions that its procedures be revised to safeguard the rights of the accused and possibilities of meaningful appeal. As a consequence its procedures seem unfair and its treatment of dissenters from the ordinary magisterium acts of a violent nature. It would be better if the CDF asked various bishops' conferences that have evolved respected procedures to look into these matters and abided by decisions made at the regional level.[5]

Some congregations in all instances and the rest in most instances truly serve the Church well. They make possible things which could not take place if the Church were simply a collection of local churches: for example, the bilateral dialogues such as Anglican Roman Catholic International Commission (ARCIC) which occur at the world level. Seemingly arbitrary and unfair interventions by some congregations, however, have seriously eroded respect for the Roman primacy in the United States and elsewhere. It is time for some congregations to become less intrusive and even cultivate a certain hesitancy to interfere.[6]

Finally, there is the issue of infallibility. Over the course of a century there has been an increasing problem of "creeping infallibilism." The declared and defined faith of the Church has been conflated with all manner of teaching, especially whatever has its source in Rome. As a consequence the distinction between the teaching of the extraordinary magisterium (solemn pronouncements of councils and popes) and that of the ordinary has been blurred. Statements by the ordinary magisterium are frequently treated as if they are subject to no change or criticism. This "creeping infallibilism" has bred its own reaction in the Church—a minimalizing tendency that says teachings of the pope and bishops need not be heeded and given respect if they are not infallible. The problem with both attitudes is that the solemn definitions of the Church do not come out of nowhere. They emerge first as ordinary teachings, are molded by the critical questions these raise, and, after much debate and revision, become suitable candidates for solemn definition.

Infallibility understood as "immunity from error" is what we have earlier called a structural reality. It sets boundaries around definition. Such an exercise of authority is quite legitimate, but it loses its life unless infallibility

---

[5] The CDF in its recent *Instructions on the Ecclesial Vocation of the Theologian* (Vatican City: Libreria Editrice Vaticana, 1990) approaches the issue of dissenting theologians in a section entitled "The Problem of Dissent." The section envisions no positive role for public dissent by a theologian from any magisterial pronouncement.

[6] Dulles, "Authority, the Divided Legacy"; Bernard Cooke, "The Vatican and the U.S. Church," *America* (October 18, 1986) 206–08.

is understood against the background of the indefectibility of the Church—its assurance that it will never become so immersed in error that it loses touch with its founder and Lord. The Church lives and does its truth. Just as individuals, as they grow to maturity, learn that things about which they were certain come to be deemed wrong, but remain confident that the true things they know both outnumber and will correct those ideas which are mistaken, the Church likewise proceeds along the self-correcting process of its pilgrim way. This way constitutes the Church's being in the truth. The Church needs to be ever ready to be reformed, that is, to ask critical questions about what it believes and does, to pass through the anguish of uncertainty and self-doubt, and to progress toward better formulations of its faith and more Christ-like ways of behaving towards its own members and its fellow travelers along the road towards peace and justice. Infallibility is a rare occurrence in this journey and occurs only in a Church which is living and thinking a self-correcting truth.[7]

The Faithful in the Church

All the baptized are authorized to proclaim the Word boldly and participate actively in the Eucharist. It is the local community which celebrates the Eucharist and the body faithful as a whole who share in the priesthood of Jesus Christ. To paraphrase Bishop de Smedt at Vatican II, the greatest day in the life of the pope is not the day on which he was ordained a priest, not the day on which he was consecrated bishop, nor the day on which he was elected to the papacy, but the day on which he was baptized. In baptism all are called to holiness and endowed with the gifts of the Holy Spirit. After baptism all enter into communion with Jesus Christ, and through him with God, and are empowered by the Spirit to live in union with all of the other baptized.

The theological virtues of faith, hope, and charity, the principal gifts at baptism, need to be appropriated over and over again. The baptized struggle so that these gifts may take firm and deeper root in their spirits. The theological reflection of the Church draws upon, challenges, and aids in the appropriation of these virtues. The orthodox faith of the Church is forged in this interplay among the active living of faith, hope, and charity, theological reflection, and pastoral teaching. For this reason orthodoxy is the concern of all.

[7] Sebastian Moore, "The Infallible Temptation," *Commonweal* (October 10, 1986) 525–27; Luis Bernejo, *Towards Christian Reunion* (Anand, India: Gujaret Shaitya Prakish, 1984); Vincent Cooke, "Hans Küng on Propositions and Their Problematic: A Critique," *The Thomist* 39 (1975) 753–65.

In the tradition of the Church the sense of the faithful occupies an honored place. It is honored as a God-given inclination for divinely revealed truth. The faithful discern the word of God even while they are simultaneously discerned by it. The sense of the faithful, when it is universal and joined to the teaching of the pastors, is considered an unerring guide to God's truth.

The sense of the faithful is not a kind of super-magisterium. It is an aspect of ecclesial reception of the faith. Sometimes it is a passive process. The faithful receive what is taught by the episcopal or papal magisteria. Always it is an active process. The people receive what is taught as responsible agents molding that faith as they proclaim it in word and deed. On occasion they contest what is taught, correcting their pastors so that the latter teach what accords with Spirit-inspired sense.

Nor is the sense of the faithful uninformed public opinion. Its discovery involves not an examination of statistics provided by public polling, but an ecclesial discernment. The Church looks to the quality and motivation of the witnesses in this process: are their opinions the consequence of prayerful faith and responsible discernment?[8]

Sometimes the sense of the faithful finds itself in opposition to the official teaching of the magisterium. What is it to do in such a situation? When anyone considers the possibility of dissent a certain caution is called for. Common sense teaches that we are loathe to criticize sufficiently our own personal assumptions or those of the secular societies in which most of us live. Too often we have learned from experience that we have tailored the gospel to our own personal needs or the accepted norms of our social group. Thus, easy dissent is an action which leads to nothing Christian. History also teaches us that numerous authentic developments in the Church have met with initial hostility from the Church at large and even from the magisterium. So, on the other hand, a facile acquiescence to what is officially taught is not necessarily the appropriate response.

The American bishops have suggested three characteristics that ought to guide any dissent from official teaching which makes no claim to be irreformable. The dissenter should show respect for the teaching office, avoid scandalizing those who have less expertise in the matters involved, and have serious reasons for one's dissent.[9] Those who would dissent should

---

[8] Avery Dulles, "Sensus Fidelium," *America* (November 1, 1986) 240–42 and 263.

[9] The American bishops have spelled out in detail their reflections on this matter. Cf. "Bishops and Theologians: Promoting Cooperation, Resolving Misunderstandings," *Origins* 19 (1989) 97, 99–110. These criteria were earlier adumbrated in *Human Life in Our Day*.

also realize that a person involved in Christian discernment will be prepared to assess critically one's own conclusions, to show reluctance to conclude that another is in error, and to conduct oneself in the public forum in a manner that reveals respect for all the parties involved.

I would like to suggest here a process which might guide anyone who is contemplating dissent from an official teaching of the Church. First of all, one should give appropriate study to the matter. This means more than reading newspaper reports. Minimally one should read an accurate rendition of what the official teacher has said. In any controverted matter there are usually contributions of experts on the question. Both support for the official teaching and arguments against it should be consulted. Obviously, the quality and extent of education plus the personal competence of the one considering dissent loom large in such study. One needs simultaneously to be humble in the face of what is not known, but forthright in using one's powers fully. This first duty, to study the matter, is requisite if the dissenter is to have serious reasons for the dissent. For dissent to be a Catholic act it must be preceded by a serious effort to convince oneself of the truth of what has been authoritatively taught (the amount of effort being proportionate to the degree of authority exercised in any particular case).

Secondly, one should pray over the matter. Prayer places us in the presence of God and relativizes both our own egoism and our insertion into secular society. It makes our decision a choice before God and not a giving in to our worst instincts or going along with the crowd. This prayer should be biblically based so that one is nurtured on the Christian story and the virtues it commends.

Third, one ought to consult other members of the Church who exhibit exemplary lives and trustworthy opinions. Here belonging to a basic community, a bible study group, or some other regular gathering of friends in the Lord can be of great help, for then conversations are carried on in the context of a history of discerning God's will together. In any event the consultations should be with persons who can be counted on to challenge self-serving intuitions, provide fresh ideas and avenues of approach, and encourage us to make a free if lonely choice.

Fourth, the formal decision process can now begin. One needs here to go over what has been studied, prayed over, and learned from friends. One might jot down the pros and cons for or against the teaching. What one looks for is the quality of what has been said. Two or three weighty arguments should be preferred to a dozen weaker ones. Eventually one will come to a decision—a decision which should be initially regarded as provisional. It may appear that more study, prayer, or consultation is called for. We also need to leave some time for ourselves to live that decision under the tutelage of the Spirit. Experience teaches us that some of our most cherished and, at the time, certain decisions are undone by life. If we have done whatever study, prayer, and consultation is necessary (here the issue at stake will dictate how much is necessary) and have discovered that the provisionary decision has proved life-giving and fulfilling, we may safely follow the lead of our discernment even if that requires dissent in word or deed from some official teaching of the Church.

On Religious Freedom

The moral claim of the baptized person is original; the claims of Church jurisdiction are derivative, that is, subordinate to the claims of the individual believer and enlisted in support of these claims. There is a great need in the Roman Catholic Church for all to accept that the use of force, whether that force is physical, psychological, or moral, almost inevitably results in an abuse of Christian conscience. Persuasion towards consensus ought to be the rule that governs living the faith of the Church. The Church ought to be the place where unprejudiced and open discussion of issues is the norm.

The religious freedom of the individual conscience *within* the Church is the principal unfinished business of the post-Vatican II Church. Following the lines of The Declaration on Religious Liberty, we might speak of the religious freedom of all the baptized as a formally juridical right: it renders each Christian immune from ecclesiastical coercion such that the individual conscience is guaranteed immunity from constraint in believing according to one's best lights and from restraint in acting according to one's beliefs. The jurisdiction of the Church is limited by the superior order of the rights and dignity of the baptized and has as its *raison d'être* the protection and vindication of those rights and that dignity. While that jurisdiction can set outside limits to the sphere in which such belief and action operate, its function is more to guarantee this sphere from forcible intrusion from without, whether that intrusion be secular or ecclesiastical.

When can an ecclesiastical jurisdictional entity intervene? Only when the public order of the Church is at stake. When does such a situation obtain? Only when what is at stake is what is necessary for the sheer coexistence of Church members within conditions of elemental Church order. Such necessity is to be sharply distinguished from what is useful to promote the collaboration of Church members toward more perfect conditions of Church welfare or to inspire their fuller participation in the benefits of Church life. While Church authorities have a duty to actualize belief, profession of the faith, and practice, they cannot invoke that duty as a basis for contravening the belief, or action based thereon, of an individual baptized believer. Only where the public order is violated, that is, the necessary conditions for Church existence are contravened or the pillars of the Church are imperiled by public dissent or a public offense, is the use of Church jurisdiction as force against an individual member justified and justifiable. The public order of the Church comprises three elements: (1) the protection of the public peace against serious disturbance; (2) the safeguarding of public morality—that minimum of realizable public morality whose maintenance is the just requirement of Church members—against serious violation; (3) the vindication of the common rights of all the baptized against trespass.

Whenever an ecclesiastical office invokes its jurisdiction to intervene and brings coercion to bear on an individual member's right to believe and act on that belief, the office bears the burden of proving that its action is justified. And it must be prepared to make that proof in the public arena according to the criteria of public Church order (and not simply according to any legal entitlement of office).

Subsequent to the council, John Courtney Murray outlined a rationale for The Declaration on Religious Liberty. We might follow his line of argument and assert that every baptized person has a right and a duty to conform the judgments of his or her conscience to the imperatives of the order of truth and to conform his or her external actions with the inner imperatives of conscience. Such responsible agency presumes, first of all, personal autonomy: that the search for the meaning of human existence, pursued in free communion with others, be subject only to the rules that govern the order of truth. It also assumes that moral worth attaches only to acts done deliberately and freely and can never be bestowed by an external agency; hence, personal judgment and choice are irreplaceable. Finally, responsible agency is inviolable and requires that the baptized person as a moral subject be responsible for its own existence. For that reason, it must be surrounded by conditions which allow room for freedom. Where the meaning of human existence and the pursuit of it, that is, the religious quest, are involved, the baptized person possesses a fundamental moral claim on others. The dignity of the baptized requires an ability to act on one's own initiative and with responsibility. This requirement is permanent, irradicable, and begets a right to immunity from coercion concerning matters religious in any juridical order, including that of the Church.[10]

In the U.S. Church today the issue of religious liberty is often transmuted into the problem of free speech in the Church, especially the rights

---

[10] John Courtney Murray, "The Declaration on Religious Freedom: A Moment in Its Legislative History," *Religious Liberty,* ed. John Courtney Murray (N.Y.: Macmillan, 1966) 15–42.

and protections of those who dissent from official teaching or policy. Here U.S. Catholics need to avoid two pitfalls. First of all they must take notice that defenses of political free speech in our nation have increasingly depended on libertarian and/or utilitarian arguments. Such arguments have seldom acknowledged any limits for or boundaries of free speech. Nothing spoken seems to be unacceptable—not in good taste perhaps, but always permissible. Furthermore, utilitarian and libertarian justifications generally betray an unwillingness to articulate any constituent elements of the public order that responsible free speakers ought to respect. The second pitfall arises from an excessive concern for orthodoxy. Hyperorthodoxy pays little heed to the fact that the allegiance to doctrine that our faith exacts requires the development of a broad consensus on what are the substantials of our creed. Being convinced that one is right is an invitation to persuade others to that rectitude and not an obligation to coerce any naysayers. There exists a crucial and necessary distinction between the minimum requirements of the true faith, required behavior, and public order and the plenitude of the faith, morality, and order that we strive together to build in a community of hope. Church government cannot be expected to root our every vice or theological taint.

Thus the Church endeavors in regard to free speech to steer a course between denial of rights in ecclesiastical procedures taken for granted in the political sphere and a passion for correctness that ignores a decent respect for the rights of dissenters in the name of Church order. Catholics cannot be articulate citizens in politics and passive recipients of Church teaching at the same time. The healthy Church order we require recognizes that a utopia where virtue reigns supreme and vice has disappeared is illusory.

By virtue of their baptism all Catholics are empowered to participate in the construction and maintenance of a Church which functions as an ordered conversation among divergent but equal partners, ever concerned that no Church member be disenfranchised from the conversation. This conversation is ordered in the sense that those who dialogue respect the rights of others and the needs of public order. Its partners can be individuals or groups as long as they act and speak as moral agents—at once free and responsible.

People who exercise authority in the Church, then, are summoned to facilitate this dialogue which explores how divine salvation will be visited upon our world today. The foundation for this dialogue is the tradition which has brought us here. Catholics are to be invited to create, build up, maintain, and renew the Church as they discuss the truths and goods that we hold in common or ought to pursue. Only if the People of God can speak freely, and are encouraged to do so responsibly (that is, respect the rights of the other and the needs of public order), will the Church flourish as a conversation.

A corollary to this concept of the Church as a dialogue about salvation is that the need to know is, in principle, unlimited. Members of the Church should receive whatever information they need for informed conversation. Limits on the dissemination of such information require public justification.

In this world, where Catholics are not only saintly, but also sinners, correction is sometimes and unfortunately necessary. Any intervening authority, however, will keep two maxims in mind. The goal of intervention is to preserve as much freedom in the Church as possible while using as little coercion as necessary. And the fostering of free inquiry into the nature of the faith and its appropriate morality is a primary duty of the magisterium.

Constraint of free speech in the Church must always be for the sake of better dialogue. The needs of public order or of respect for others' rights must be publicly demonstrated (or demonstrable). No simple solution, applicable in all cases, to controversies over what to say in the Lord exists. Differences in culture, country, circumstances, or times require careful scrutiny. Any process of Church censorship must of its nature be formally juridical with the premises and objectives clearly defined. And the actual workings of those processes over time needs to be sustained by the broad consent of the faithful.

Anyone who would engage in censorship must realize that censorship is always an exception to the rule which calls those irresponsible in speech back to the wisdom of the Church. This wisdom flourishes in a community where persons are by and large presumed to be morally and socially responsible and prudent in their use of freedom of expression.[11]

> The attitude of opposition is a function, on the one hand, of that particular view one takes of the community and of what is good for it, and on the other, of the strong need to participate in the common existing and even more so in the common acting. There can be no doubt that this kind of opposition is essentially constructive; it is a condition of the correct structure of communi-

[11] John Coleman, "John Courtney Murray and 'The Other' First Amendment," (to be published in a collection of essays on Murray from Notre Dame Press); see also John C. Murray, "Freedom, Authority, Community," *America* 115 (December 3, 1966) 734–41; "Freedom in the Age of Renewal," *American Benedictine Review* 18 (September 1967) 319–24; "We Held These Truths," *National Catholic Reporter* (November 23, 1967); and "The Will to Community," *Theological Freedom And Social Responsibility,* ed. Stephen Bayne (N.Y.: Seabury, 1967) 112–16.

ties and of the correct functioning of their inner system. This condition, however, must be defined more precisely: the structure, the system of communities, must be such as to allow the opposition that grows out of the soil of solidarity not only to express itself within the framework of the community but also to operate for the benefit of the community—to be constructive. The structure of human community is correct only if it admits not just the presence of a justified opposition but also that effectiveness of opposition which is required by the common good and the right of participation.[12]

---

[12] Karol Wojtyla, *The Active Person,* trans. Andrzej Potocki (London: D. Reidel, 1979) 286.

Index